In loving memory of my mom,
Koushalya Kishnani

COHERENT COMMUNICATION

*A Step-by-Step Guide to
Being an Ally to Yourself and Others*

Mona Kishnani Johnson

Kishnani Empowerment Center
Redwood City, CA 94063

© 2025 by Mona Kishnani Johnson

All rights reserved, including the right to reproduce this book or portions of this book in any form whatsoever, without the prior written permission of the copyright owner.

Library of Congress Control Number: 2025914411

ISBN 97989993985-0-5 (Paperback)
ISBN 97989993985-8-1 (ebook)

The author of this book does not dispense medical advice or prescribe the use of any technique as a form of treatment for physical, emotional, or medical problems without the advice of a physician, either directly or indirectly. The author is not a doctor or a mental health professional. The intent of the author is to offer information to help you in your quest for empowerment. It is your responsibility to seek appropriate help.

To my dad and mom for their enduring love and dedication to their children.

To all the humans who are dedicated to being their authentic selves, living their truth, following their passion, and creating a peaceful, fun, and thriving planet through joyous service.

CONTENTS

Preface ix
Special Thanks xv
Introduction xvii
Part I 1
    How to Be an Ally to Oneself 3
    Spiritual Domain 7
    Emotional Domain 16
    Mental Domain 25
    Physical Domain 45
    Part I Summary 57
Part II 67
    Ten Techniques to Become an Ally to Others 72
    Part II Summary 101
Conclusion 107
References 111
Early Testimonials 115

PREFACE

After working in the corporate world for twenty-five years and facing two layoffs and one dismissal, I decided to take six months to nurture my family and my own well-being and to write and publish my first book, *The Power of Universal Laws: A Parent/Teacher Guide to Raising Empowered Children in Four Stages.*

After about six months of time off, I started applying and interviewing for opportunities. During my interview process with various corporations, I heard the same questions: "How do you deal with difficult personalities? How do you deal with conflict, change, and crisis? How do you deal with uncertainty?" I wondered why the challenge of communication is constant in our lives and societies. A vast majority of conflicts, misunderstandings, and challenges can be resolved through communication. But why is there so much conflict in the world at all levels—intrapersonal, interpersonal, home, workplace, society, governments, and within and between countries?

PREFACE

I pondered the many corporate training courses on effective communication that I had participated in or organized. I had gained nuggets of wisdom along the way, but none of them sunk deep into my consciousness to make an impact and bring about permanent behavioral change. They made sense at a rational mind level but felt superficial. Soon after the gruesome murder of George Floyd, an African American man, that resulted in nationwide protests in 2020, corporations could no longer stay quiet regarding the injustices happening in the environment around them. The company I was working for organized a training course called "How to Be an Ally to Others." Although it seemed well-intentioned, I felt something deep was missing. I wondered how we can be allies to others when we don't feel safe enough to be our own authentic selves, instead wearing masks to please others and to fit into corporate culture. How can we be allies to others when we don't know how to be allies to ourselves because we have not taken stock of who we really are or assessed our values? The answer is simple. In our homes, educational institutions, cultures, workplaces, and societies where we grew up, how to be an ally to others wasn't taught or role modeled to us.

Researching how to create high-performing teams, Google concluded that creating psychological safety in which team members feel safe to express themselves is key (Duhigg, 2016). When team members feel safe to express themselves and be authentic, they are their most creative selves. When they are their most creative selves, effective solutions to challenges and problems emerge, allowing creativity and innovation to flow. The team member feels empowered to be their

PREFACE

authentic self without hiding behind a persona—a mask—out of fear of being singled out, rejected, or losing their livelihood. Each team member feeling empowered serves as the foundation of a high-performing team that can respond to any challenge with creative solutions.

I pondered whether psychological safety is possible and who is responsible for creating it. Is it the leader's responsibility to create psychological safety? What if the leader is unaware of or does not know how to create psychological safety?

I had a breakthrough regarding some of these questions when I obtained my spiritual life coaching certification at the Holistic Learning Center and my Building Personal Resilience Mentor Certification at the HeartMath Institute. My training as a life coach and practitioner of building personal resilience taught me that the solution lies within *me*. It is the individual's responsibility to create their own psychological safety. The key to the creation of psychological safety is to learn how to first be an ally to oneself. It begins by taking accountability for first being allies and best friends to ourselves before we can be allies to others or expect others to be allies to us. Some of the benefits of first being an ally to oneself include the following:

1. Our capacity to be resilient increases, because we have a greater capacity to prepare for, deal with, and respond to life challenges with grace, courage, and ability.

2. We can be our authentic, creative, and unique selves living from our truth.

3. We can co-create and shape our realities based on our inner genius, leading to more fulfilling lives.

By being allies to ourselves first, we learn to empathize and put ourselves in others' shoes to elevate communication with the interests of both parties in mind. We offer the same grace to others as we would offer ourselves. Here are some benefits of being an ally to others:

1. Arguments, disagreements, and conflicts get resolved peacefully.

2. Relationships deepen.

3. Creative solutions to challenges emerge.

4. Satisfaction, engagement, and productivity increase at home and in the workplace.

I term the symbiotic relationship between being an ally to oneself and being an ally to others *coherent communication*. This means that we communicate from a space where our emotions, minds, and hearts are in sync. Physiologically, it means that the physical systems, our hormonal systems, and our autonomous nervous systems are working in sync. I

PREFACE

will explore the definition of coherent communication in more depth in the introduction.

This book is divided into two parts, with Part I exploring how to be an ally to oneself and Part II exploring techniques of coherent communication for being an ally to others. I leverage the wisdom of the Universal Laws—the laws through which we evolve and grow (Johnson, 2023). I share examples from my personal life and my coaching practice, while upholding client confidentiality, to capture the essence and application of the tools and techniques. I use the words *coherence* and *empowerment* interchangeably, as I believe that coherence leads to psychological safety, which in turn leads to empowerment. Part I is extensive because I believe self-allyship is a crucial foundation for building strong and meaningful connections with others.

SPECIAL THANKS

Thank you to Master Coach Hu Dalconzo and the Holistic Learning Center where I obtained my spiritual life coaching certification. Thank you for teaching me tools to bring awareness to my limiting beliefs.

I am grateful to HeartMath Institute where I obtained my Resilience Training Certification. Thank you for introducing heart coherence techniques for tapping into the infinite wisdom of the heart.

Thank you to Cheryl Roberts Oliver and Nicole Guenther for editing this book with love.

I give special thanks to my mentor, Kara Goss, for guiding and encouraging me to follow my heart and for embodying the universal truths of being an ally to myself and others.

Finally, thank you to my loving husband and daughter for inspiring me each day and embracing me for who I am.

INTRODUCTION

What is coherent communication? As mentioned briefly in the preface, coherent communication originates from deep within. It means that we are not reacting from a space of fight or flight where our nervous and hormonal systems are not synchronized. It means we are connecting with and communicating from the deep intelligence of our hearts. HeartMath Institute teaches: "Every life has its challenges. Every heart has an answer." When I studied with HeartMath Institute, I learned about the infinite intelligence and intuitive guidance of the heart—called "heart coherence" or "inner battery"—as the metaphor for resilience capacity. I refer to it as our *inner guidance system* or our *inner empowerment battery*, full of vital life force energy to support us in navigating life challenges and adversities and leading authentic and fulfilling lives. Most spiritual texts I have read and myths I know point to the infinite wisdom, love, intelligence, and compassion of this inner guidance system. Please substitute whatever word or phrase you associate with the inner guidance system—Jesus Christ, Allah,

INTRODUCTION

Buddha, Shakti, Universal Intelligence, Universal Life Force Energy, God Intelligence, Namaste Consciousness, One Consciousness, Unity Consciousness, I AM Consciousness, Divine Consciousness, Love, etc. I use the phrase Universal-Self.

The inner guidance system—my Universal-Self—reminds me of a time when my family moved into a townhome with a two-car garage. I was thrilled at the prospect of having a designated parking space after years of street parking. But when I went to park the family car, I realized the garage was too narrow. The car had to be at the exact right angle to fit without busting the side mirrors or dinging the car. My excitement turned into anxiety each time I had to pull the car into and out of the garage. I ended up denting the car and, in one instance, busting one of the side mirrors, which cost over $2000 to repair. One day, when adjusting the side mirrors, I accidentally pushed a button that folded the side mirrors in. I hadn't known this feature existed. I now use the folding mirrors feature each time I pull into the garage, parking the car without anxiety. It works like a charm.

On reflection, I realized that the solution had existed all along within the car, and I just had to be aware of the feature. I smiled to myself, thinking, *If you had been a better driver, you would have read the car manual and been informed about the feature*. In fact, only when I faced the challenge and had to go looking for solutions did I become aware of the feature.

This is a metaphor for life. When faced with suffering and pain, we look for comfort and solace. Creative solutions to our dilemmas exist within us. We need to be aware of and tap into the innate infinite guidance and wisdom that lies within us by being coherent (empowered) in each of the four interrelated domains of our lives:

1. **Physical domain coherence:** We have healthy, vibrant bodies.

2. **Emotional domain coherence:** We are mature enough to regulate our emotions and maintain a positive outlook.

3. **Mental domain coherence:** We have empowering thoughts and behaviors, and we are wise in our actions.

4. **Spiritual domain coherence:** We're our authentic, peaceful, creative selves and tolerant of others' values and beliefs.

When we act from the combination of these powers, we have the best chance of tapping into our innate guidance system full of vital life force energy. We feel psychologically safe in our bodies to be our authentic selves and can respond to challenges and adversities with grace and ability. We offer the same sense of psychological safety to others wherever we go. We are fully present in our communication and interactions. We realize that we are all connected at a deeper level through this innate guidance system. We are our strongest ally. We are not inadvertently draining the vital life force energy of our inner empowerment battery. We tap into the power of our inner empowerment battery to co-create the realities we desire. By being strong allies to ourselves, we become allies to others as well.

However, under stressful situations when we are experiencing emotions like anger and frustration, or subtle emotions like worry or depression, we may unconsciously disconnect from our inner guidance system. Our hearts become incoherent. This sends a chaotic signal to the brain that impacts our mental domain—our brain's ability to process information, make decisions, solve problems, and engage in discernment and creativity. Physiologically, stress hormones increase, impacting our physical domain. We feel exhausted, and our ability to think clearly diminishes. Our inner empowerment battery is drained. We do not feel psychologically safe to show up as our authentic selves. Our communication suffers, because we are not fully present in our interactions, and we are not our authentic selves. This impacts relationships with ourself, our loved ones, our coworkers, and society at large.

Therefore, the foundation for coherent communication lies in our being coherent and empowered in each of our interrelated domains (spiritual, emotional, mental, and physical) supporting us to fully connect to, identify with, and trust our inner guidance system—our Universal-Self—completely. This helps us be fully present, communicate with our coherent heart, and be in full communion with the other person.

PART I

Part I explores deep realizations, tools, and resources on how to first be an ally to oneself by becoming empowered in each of the four interrelated domains. So what does it mean to be an ally to oneself?

Have you witnessed how you communicate with yourself? Hit the pause button and witness the self-talk happening in the background. Is it a constant stream of fears, judgments of ourselves and others, insecurities, anxieties, or feeling unsafe, uncomfortable, and uncertain? Or does the self-talk originate from a feeling of peace, love, expansion, openness, curiosity, and eagerness to learn and grow? When we are preoccupied with conflicting communication in the background, we are not fully present with our surroundings, ourselves, our loved ones, our coworkers, and everyone we interact with on a day-to-day basis. How can we form deep relationships and connections when most of our time is consumed by self-talk, opinions, judgments, fears, and prejudices that inadvertently drain our inner empowerment battery? It sometimes feels like we're operating as zombies on autopilot, blurting out our responses and reactions based on our programming, sometimes while the other person is still speaking.

Being an ally to oneself means demonstrating love, compassion, understanding, empathy, and forgiveness to oneself first. When we learn to accept and love ourselves with all our imperfections and perfections, we start freeing ourselves of the constant stream of self-limiting talk, prejudices, opinions, and fears operating our lives in the background. We have a deep realization that we are always learning and growing through trial and error. We learn to forgive ourselves for all the errors we make, we own our errors, we learn and evolve from them, and we make empowered choices. We feel psychologically safe to be our authentic selves and communicate from our uniqueness and power: the power that connects us to the infinite intelligence and coherence of our hearts—our Universal-Self. We become our authentic selves and tap into our inner genius. We possess the ability to put ourselves in the shoes of others and be fully present in each communication and interaction. We transform into safe space holders of coherent communication. We learn to offer grace to others and be their ally. After all, we can only give others what we already possess.

HOW TO BE AN ALLY TO ONESELF

To be allies to ourselves, we are first responsible for being coherent in each of the four interrelated domains of our lives: spiritual, emotional, mental, and physical. When we are coherent in each of the four domains, then our hearts, emotions, minds, nervous systems, and hormonal systems are in sync, and we are connected to the inner guidance system that is all-knowing, infinite, compassionate, and all-truth. When we identify and build a trusting relationship with the inner guidance system, we receive the guidance to show up as the best version of ourselves.

Therefore, we are responsible for taking care of ourselves in all four domains:

1. **Spiritually** through prayer, meditation, and connecting to creativity.

2. **Emotionally** through balancing our emotions.

3. **Mentally** through kindness, compassion, and empowering thoughts.

4. **Physically** through diet, nutrition, exercise, and empowering actions.

With consistent nurturing practices in each of our four domains, we are connected to the unlimited energy reserves of our Universal-Self—our inner empowerment battery. My view of this is an interdependent relationship with our Universal-Self. We are co-creators of our life with our Universal-Self in the front seat, and we have the resilience to respond to life challenges and adversities with grace and ability.

Before we dive into tools for developing coherence in each of the domains, there is one underlying truth that ties together the performance of all the domains, and it is this: Our underlying beliefs, conscious or unconscious, create our reality. Scientists estimate that up to 95 percent of our beliefs are unconscious (Morse, 2002). Deep programming of our belief systems, positive and negative, starts from the time we are born. Our subconscious minds are constantly fed programming by our caretakers, educational institutions, governments, entertainment channels, social media, news channels, and environment. We absorb all the programming without judging or reasoning whether it is relevant and empowering for us. Our mind unconsciously downloads and replays the subconscious programming and belief systems; therefore, we repeatedly recreate the same life situations and lessons that are often painful without understanding why.

For example, I used to feel defensive and sensitive when my loved ones, friends, coworkers, or managers corrected me. I felt as though I was constantly being scrutinized and criticized. I questioned why, out of the hundreds of things I did well, everyone harped on the one thing I should be doing better. I felt unappreciated. I became combative and started pointing out flaws in them. The anger and frustration I was feeling were unconsciously draining the vital life force energy from my empowerment battery in my emotional domain. Mentally, I felt less motivated. Physically, I felt drained and turned to food for comfort. Spiritually, I felt disconnected, because I did not have the energy to connect to my inner guidance system—my Universal-Self. It felt like a reactionary cycle.

Through my life coaching certification training, I was able to consider my feelings and became aware that my mind was inwardly propagating the lie: "I am not capable or talented enough." Something was missing. Unknowingly, I criticized and judged myself. The outside world reflected the internal criticism. Taking the time to witness the narrative of my mind and to listen to and embrace the judgmental feelings about myself led me to an empowering choice to value, love, and embrace myself. This was a liberating discovery. My affirmation to myself that I internalized and emotionalized is "I am capable and talented enough. I am priceless. I offer something of worth. Every day, I learn and develop. I do not need outside approval anymore. I am receptive to constructive feedback that is meant to improve me, without taking it personally. I am my strongest ally."

We bump into our unconscious beliefs in any of the domains through our thoughts, words, feelings, and actions. Therefore, it is important to be aware and take stock of our limiting unconscious beliefs, then work at dis-creating them and replacing them with empowering beliefs.

I review the mechanics of dis-creating limiting beliefs and replacing them with empowering beliefs in the physical domain. Although I share tools for getting coherent in each of the domains, many of the tools overlap and can be used across domains, as all the domains are interrelated and impact each other.

SPIRITUAL DOMAIN

The spiritual domain sets the foundation for and informs all the domains. Coherence in this domain serves as a North Star to coherence in other domains. As mentioned in the introduction, the fundamental truth is that we are all connected to the infinite intelligence and compassion of an innate guidance system through our spiritual domain. We are unique manifestations of this guidance system with our unique abilities and strengths. This guidance system is beyond the rational limited guidance of our minds.

I have witnessed personally and in my clients that unconscious negative beliefs in this domain have a ripple effect on all the other domains. This leads to incoherence, disconnection from our internal guidance system, and depletion of our empowerment battery and consequently results in a lack of optimal performance of the four domains.

Our biggest unconscious negative belief is that we are raised to believe, through endless generations of fear-based programming, that we are separate from our Universal-Self and from each other. We are raised to believe that we are weak in body and mind. Our connection to the infinite internal guidance system dispels this belief by stating that our Universal-Self (our innate guidance system with its infinite intelligence, powers, and life force energy) and ourselves "are one" and that everything in the universe is "intrinsically connected, irrevocably interdependent, interactive, and interwoven into the fabric of all life" (Walsch, 2005).

When we take the time to connect to this innate guidance system, we feel secure in who we are—we are our authentic selves and not the selves that the external programming of our environment teaches us to be. We are not trying to fit any mold to be accepted by others and please others. We are not seeking external validation. We know what is important to us and what our passions and values are. We are true to our uniqueness. We discover that we are the spark of the divine system, that we are *spirit* first with a mind and a body, and that we have the innate ability to use the limitless energy reserves of our guidance system to co-create the reality we desire and deserve. Leonardo Di Vinci serves as an inspiring example of someone with a strong connection to his Universal-Self, the innate guidance system; this Italian polymath of the High Renaissance used his life force energy reserves as a painter, draftsman, engineer, scientist, theorist, sculptor, and architect (Kemp, 2003).

In addition, we realize that we are all one in *spirit*. Thanks to centuries of discoveries in quantum physics, we are learning to understand that at the fundamental level, nature, the universe, and everything around us is made up of electrons and photons. According to Neil deGrasse Tyson, an American astrophysicist, author, and science communicator, "We are all connected; To each other, biologically. To the earth, chemically. To the rest of the universe atomically." He states, "We are in the universe and the universe is in us" (Goodreads). Similarly, scientists at Caltech discuss the topic of quantum physics, saying, "Quantum science may even reveal how everything in the universe (or in multiple universes) is connected to everything else through higher dimensions that our senses cannot comprehend" (Caltech, 2023).

Listed below are some of the fundamental truths that guide us as we connect to our spiritual domain. Studying, practicing, internalizing, and emotionalizing these truths each day guides us in being our own best allies as we steer our lifeboat on the river of life. The Sanskrit term for this interconnection is "Namaste Consciousness," which means "The God in me honors the God in you." Master Coach Hu Dalconzo, the founder of the Holistic Learning Center, adds to this definition, saying, "I honor the place in you, which is of truth, light, peace and love! And when we communicate with that level of awareness, we are One!" (1998, p. 1). We are transformed. Dalconzo continued, "Trans-form-ation means 'to go beyond form' to a level of conscious understanding that the real you exists beyond the physical form of your human body" (Dalconzo, 2016b, p. 87). We are aware of the limited nature of our physical body and our limited time on earth. We live each day with an important question running in the background: What will our legacy be when we are no more? Will it be a legacy of peace and love or a legacy of chaos and conflict? We are coherent in our communication when we are guided by the answer to this important question.

When I coach clients, we excavate and dis-create unconscious negative beliefs related to a lack of awareness of the following seven fundamental truths and identify with our innate guidance system—our Universal-Self.

The first fundamental truth is that *we are never alone.* Our innate guidance system, with its infinite intelligence and life force energy, is always with us. It is part of our divine heritage. This same life force energy makes our hearts beat, makes us breathe effortlessly, helps us digest our food, creates babies, drives our cars while we are engaged in conversations, connects us telepathically to our friends and people, inspires us with ideas, and prompts us to take action. With its infinite organizing and correlational powers, it supports us as we navigate through our life challenges and as we co-create what we desire. By taking the time daily to connect to the guidance system, we feel psychologically safe and secure, and we learn to build our trust in this guidance system. We share all our struggles, trials, and tribulations along with what we desire. We learn to receive guidance at opportune times. This trust in our inner guidance system builds energy reserves in our empowerment battery and empowers us to co-create our reality.

The next truth is to *love and accept ourselves.* As we take the time to build the connection and identify with the innate guidance system, we realize that each one of us is a unique manifestation of this guidance system. There is only one of us with our unique energy signature in the whole of the universe—our unique combination of electrons and photons vibrating at a frequency. Sure, we have our areas for improvement and our strengths. We learn to accept all of ourselves with all our imperfections and perfections with the realization and curiosity that we are all learning and growing each day. We take the time to dis-create any unconscious "less than others" or "not enough" negative beliefs that we are not good enough, not talented enough, not worthy enough, not wealthy enough, etc. Instead, we start to develop faith and trust in our guidance system. We reprogram ourselves with empowering beliefs that promote self-love and self-acceptance. We do not suffer from either an inferiority complex or a superiority complex because we realize that a superiority complex is just an inferiority complex in disguise (Dalconzo, 2016b). We do not drain our vital energy reserves by wearing masks and pretending to be who we truly are not. We love and accept all of ourselves.

Accepting and embracing uniqueness is the third fundamental truth. We learn to accept and embrace our uniqueness and the value we bring to the table—both our physical uniqueness and the talents, skills, and abilities we possess. We take the time to invest in our unique talents instead of being a lemming and following others or doing what others expect of us. We are aware of and feel secure in our self-worth. We embrace our inner genius.

The next truth is to *be aware of and uphold our values.* As we fully love and accept ourselves, being comfortable and secure in ourselves, we begin to be clear about what matters to us and what values we want to live by. This becomes our moral compass, supporting us as we navigate through the various ebbs and flows of our life. It becomes part of our eulogy and our legacy.

Possessing clarity of our goals and purpose and being true to our words is the next truth. When we realize our self-worth and possess self-esteem, we have clarity about our purpose and our true passions. Our words become the law of the universe, and we possess the courage to take action toward achieving our goals. We lead purposeful lives with deep realization and daily awareness about our actions and our legacy. We do not take our relationships and time for granted. Staying true to our passions and our purpose, we live each day with a sense of focus and urgency.

The sixth truth is that we need to *learn to separate ourselves from our behaviors.* We learn that we are not our behaviors and that we have functional and dysfunctional behaviors. It requires courage to lean into our experiences, witness our unconscious or conscious behaviors, take ownership, and ask the question, "What can I learn and how can I grow from this experience?" We learn to forgive ourselves and do better, which fosters a growth mindset. Maya Angelou's saying rings true: "Do the best you can until you know better. Then, when you know better, do better" (Kaiser, 2016). We realize there are no mistakes, only lessons. This frees us from draining our empowerment battery by feeling guilty about our errors and failures. Healing and transformation happen when we awaken to the realization that there is no value in attaching to and identifying with past pain and suffering. We take accountability and responsibility for our errors. We are remorseful and learn from our errors so we don't repeat them. We release our guilt. We realize that the purpose of our lives is education and not punishment of ourselves and others.

The last fundamental truth I'll mention is to *respect and avoid violating our boundaries*. As we learn to grow and identify with our uniqueness, values, beliefs, and talents, our self-esteem and confidence in our abilities grow. We learn to understand components of our boundaries: (a) our *physical* boundary is the invisible three-foot comfort zone that surrounds us to feel physically safe; (b) the *emotional* boundary is anchored deeply to our self-love, self-acceptance, self-esteem, and self-image; (c) our *mental* boundary is related to our mental clarity, focus, and interpersonal effectiveness; and (d) our *spiritual* boundary is anchored in being clear about and committed to moral values while at the same time respecting others. Healthy, mature boundaries support us to feel safe and secure in the world and not get enmeshed in other people's fear-based belief systems and values. We are aware of and use our choice to either speak up or remove ourselves from situations that violate our boundaries. By standing up for and respecting our boundaries, we send a signal to others around us that we love and respect ourselves.

Some of the tools to connect to our spiritual domain include prayer and meditation, heart coherent techniques, and connecting with creativity. According to Dalconzo, "Prayer and meditation are 'two halves of the same whole' when it comes to spiritual communication with the Universal-Self" (Dalconzo, 1998, p. 186). Carving out time each day to sit in stillness to connect with and listen to the innate guidance system through prayer and meditation promotes our sense of safety and security.

Prayer is taking the time to have a direct conversation with the Divine Consciousness—our innate guidance system where we are free to talk about anything and everything, share our deepest fears, and ask for support and guidance in navigating our life challenges and manifesting our desires.

The intention of meditation is to be fully present to the expansiveness of our Universal-Self and to listen to the answers to our prayers by quieting the constant chatter of the mind. Sitting in stillness—preferably for 15–30 minutes at the start of the day before we plunge into our busy lives, and at the end of the day before we retire for the night—helps us connect to eternal peace and be open to receive and listen to the required guidance from our Universal-Self.

Heart coherent techniques are simple, concise, and easy to integrate into our busy lives if we remember to practice every day. They are in-the-moment techniques. My clients and I use HeartMath coherent techniques as practical and effective ways to neutralize stress reactions. The techniques are helpful because it may not always be possible or practical to meditate during the middle of the workday. Heart coherent techniques build resilience by connecting to the intelligence of our hearts.

Connecting with creativity is based on the fact that each one of us is unique. We have our passions that we are fully engaged in, can focus on in the present, and find fulfillment in. Taking the time to reflect on our childhood and other times when we felt at peace and creative ideas were flowing—those

SPIRITUAL DOMAIN

moments when we were truly enjoying what we were doing—helps us stay connected to infinite, innate creative intelligence. I feel that our passions and creativity are our gateway to awareness of our unique gifts for our empowerment. For me, writing, nature walks, and yoga are my creative connections. When I do these activities, I feel connected to my Universal-Self and my empowerment battery gets replenished.

EMOTIONAL DOMAIN

Feelings in our emotional domain are one of the gateways where we receive intuitive messages from our Universal-Self, especially if we are out of alignment in our spiritual domain. Feelings are powerful tools. If we are not aware of the feelings we possess, we drain the vital energy reserves from our empowerment battery. Our feelings are not good or bad—they are comfortable or uncomfortable. They serve as guideposts, showing where we are in alignment with or out of alignment with our Universal-Self. We encounter challenges when we are programmed to block, think, and rationalize our feelings. We need to embrace, feel, process, gain wisdom from, and neutralize our feelings. For example, when feelings like anger, frustration, envy, and fear are blocked and not allowed to be felt or processed, we burn a lot of energy reserves. Subtle feelings like worry, sadness, shame, hurt, embarrassment, and disappointment run in the background as subtle energy drains in our empowerment battery.

HeartMath Institute uses the analogy that big energy drains are similar to when we suddenly floor the accelerator in our car, draining the fuel, whereas subtle energy drains are like leaving the lights on in the car after we turn off the ignition (Institute of HeartMath, 2014). The unprocessed feelings remain in our bodies as blocked emotions, depleting our empowerment battery and impacting our resilience to not only face challenges and adversities but also to lead fulfilled lives. On the other hand, when we allow ourselves to embrace and feel our comfortable and uncomfortable feelings, they impart wisdom and increase our resilience. For example, allowing ourselves to feel frustrated grants us wisdom to persist when things take longer than expected. When we block the feeling of frustration, we become judgmental of others and ourselves. Feeling scared is a normal and naturally uncomfortable feeling associated with starting something new. When we block and resist feeling scared, we immobilize ourselves and resist new experiences, often feeling confused and hopeless.

Blocked emotions impact the feeling pathways between the brain and the heart. Permanent behavioral changes occur when we change the feeling pathways between the brain and the heart (Institute of HeartMath, 2014). The amygdala, a crucial brain region for emotional experiences, is directly connected to the heart by a strong and direct nervous system pathway. Every time the heart beats, the amygdala synchronously responds. For instance, if the heart frequently experiences feelings of frustration, anxiety, tension, sadness, and/or worry, the amygdala synchronizes to the incoherent heart rhythms as "normal" and "comfortable" and establishes a feeling neural pathway that does not serve us. The amygdala strives to maintain a similar match to the signal it receives from the heart. We keep recreating the same behavioral patterns and experiences that do not serve us well.

In addition, there are hormonal responses to blocked emotions in the physical domain. When our emotions linger in our bodies for an extended period, they trigger the stress hormone cortisol that can stay in our physical systems for a long time, potentially lasting weeks, months, or even years without intervention, impacting our sleep cycle, metabolism, and immune systems. When we don't get regenerative sleep, our empowerment battery gets depleted, which has a long-term impact on our health, leading to diseases.

With this awareness and knowledge, we are empowered to embrace, feel, process, and neutralize our uncomfortable feelings that are not serving us well. We possess the ability to create new, healthier-feeling pathways that serves and empowers us by reprogramming our heart and brain with empowering beliefs by practicing more regular heart coherence, being present in the moment, being a witness to our emotions, and being in tune with our spiritual domain—our Universal-Self—more frequently and over an extended period. It is much like downloading a new operating system onto our computer or building a new foundation for a house (Institute of HeartMath, 2014). With consistent practice, we gain wisdom from unwanted attitudes, reactions, and behaviors that no longer serve us, and we replace them with healthier responses that become familiar and automatic with time.

Coherence in the emotional domain leads to the release of "feel-good" vitality hormones like oxytocin, serotonin, and DHEA (dehydroepiandrosterone), which promote the well-being of our immune system, metabolism, sleep/wake cycles, and nervous systems because we are not in fight-or-flight mode. We gain emotional maturity to validate and self-regulate our emotions, have a positive outlook on life, and be our own best ally.

Some of the tools to support resilience and coherence in the emotional domain include learning the language of feelings, feeling your feelings, using the first-party communication tool, and validating and neutralizing feelings.

Learn the Language of Feelings

When we take the time to witness, feel, embrace, and neutralize our intuitive (comfortable and uncomfortable) feelings, then what we feel is perfect for our evolution and growth. This allows us to connect with the infinite wisdom of our Universal-Self. However, when we try to think, judge, reason, reject, resist, or not acknowledge our intuitive feelings, we connect with the narrative of the ego mind, which is part of the mental domain. We are thinkaholics and spend a lot of time *thinking about* our feelings instead of *feeling* our feelings. These unprocessed feelings stay in our bodies as blocked emotions, and we unconsciously recreate our experiences based on those blocked emotions.

As mentioned under the spiritual domain, what I have found through my healing and coaching practice is that blocked emotions can sometimes be rooted in unconscious negative beliefs because of our lack of awareness and integration with the fundamental truths related to the spiritual domain. For instance, Nancy came to me angry and sad because no one in her household was listening to her. Through the coaching exercises, she learned that she did not value herself and did not keep her word and commitment to herself. Her outer world was reflecting what was happening inside herself. She understood and processed where she was out of harmony and alignment with her inner Universal-Self. Our innate guidance system communicates to us through intuitive feelings. Therefore, taking the time to sit in stillness with the uncomfortable feelings sometimes reveals to us where we are out of harmony and alignment with our inner Universal-Self.

The blocked emotions in the body can trigger a response from our nervous system, which initiates a fight-or-flight response. For example, Sharon was always in a state of high anxiety and panic. She thought that her manager and her customers were constantly judging her work and providing feedback on how she could improve. Her nervous system was on fire, and this depleted her empowerment battery, even before she arrived at work. When we worked together, we unpacked the unconscious belief that had roots in her childhood where she did not believe in her abilities and held the thought that she was not good enough. She lacked awareness and appreciation for all she accomplished. When I asked her to make a list of her accomplishments, the truth was that she had accomplished a lot in her life. She was working with a nervous system that was programmed over the years by the constant feeling of anxiety as the "normal way of operation." She was subconsciously attracting situations where people lacked appreciation for her abilities.

I unconsciously used "getting busy" and "constantly working hard" to not feel my uncomfortable feeling of anxiety. When I created space and gave myself permission to feel the uncomfortable feeling of anxiety by sitting in stillness, it imparted to me the wisdom to feel safe in my body, let go of control, and trust that all experiences are unfolding in my highest and greatest good and that my Universal-Self has my back.

The sooner we learn and master the language of feelings, the sooner we unearth our negative unconscious beliefs. Once we unearth our negative unconscious beliefs, we have the choice to stop draining our precious energy reserves, start stepping into our power to manifest our desires, and respond to life's challenges with grace and ability.

Feel Your Feelings

Years of formal education have trained us to be thinkaholics. We are trained and programmed to process our lives through our thoughts and not our feelings. Feelings exist only in the present; therefore, the only way to truly "feel" our feelings is to experience them in a vehicle that only exists in the present—our body. Being a witness, or bringing our awareness to where we feel emotion in our body, anchors the quality of our Universal-Self's presence. The mind gets caught up in the narrative of the past or the future; however, our body exists here and now, in the present moment, serving as a reminder to identify with our Universal-Self. To feel and heal our uncomfortable feelings, we must first scan our bodies and ask ourselves, "What am I truly feeling? Where am I feeling the 'uncomfortable feeling' in my body? What message does the feeling have for me? Are there any unconscious negative beliefs underlying the messages?" This supports us to truly listen and learn to distinguish between the narrative of the thinking mind where we are programmed to think, judge, reason, and analyze our feelings versus being in our bodies and asking ourselves, "Am I in my mind or in my body? What wisdom is there behind my feelings?" These questions create awareness within us to be in our bodies instead of in the constant chatter of our minds.

HeartMath Institute has a free meditation tool called "Notice and Ease" for identifying and admitting our uncomfortable negative feelings and emotions. When used, it helps prevent the drain on our empowerment battery in our emotional domain by breathing in ease and guiding us to intuitive messages and perceptions. Taking the time to sit in stillness and feel the uncomfortable feelings in my body has led me to unearth an unconscious negative belief that "I am not worthy of receiving." My ego mind always had rational excuses that I was not talented enough or not good enough. It was trying to keep me safe from the uncomfortable feeling of embarrassment. It was a liberating discovery and a reminder of self-acceptance to believe in myself, my talents, and the value I offer each day to myself, my family, my work, and my clients. My empowering belief is "I am worthy of receiving all that belongs to me in divine right."

Use First-Party Communication

I learned the first-party communication tool during my coaching certification. It is a powerful tool because it does not allow us to be unconscious about what we are feeling at the present moment. It allows us to own what we are feeling. If we don't own what we are feeling, we will not heal at a deeper unconscious level, and permanent behavioral changes will not occur. Therefore, it is important to tune into our feelings and use the first party (a first-person point of view) to write down what we are feeling: *I am feeling sad, I am feeling happy, I am feeling disappointed, I am feeling frustrated*. First-party communication unravels the excuses the ego mind provides so that we can feel safe and therefore avoid the hard and sometimes painful work it takes to allow and feel our uncomfortable feelings that are signaling to us that we are out of alignment with our Universal-Self. (I write about the workings of the ego mind under the mental domain.)

Ariana had the habit of procrastination. She was procrastinating looking for a job opportunity that fit her. When we worked together, we uncovered an unconscious belief that she felt she was not good enough. This was linked to a childhood incident of feeling hurt and confused when she felt judged and embarrassed by her dad in front of house guests. Her ego mind blocked her uncomfortable feelings of hurt, shame, and embarrassment, replacing them with the emotions of self-pity, guilt, and perfectionism, all of which provided her excuses for why she would not find "the right" job opportunity.

Validate and Neutralize the Feelings

Setting time aside to acknowledge, validate, and neutralize our uncomfortable feelings grants us permission to see and feel what happened and what we experienced in a holistic, well-grounded manner. It provides awareness and increases our consciousness, allowing us to feel and own what we feel without judgment. When we fully witness and own our feelings, a portal opens and a shift happens, creating a space to neutralize the intensity of our feelings and to make conscious, empowered choices about how we respond to the situation. We are no longer hijacked by judgment, rationalizations, excuses, and fear-based thoughts governed by the programming from our past negative experiences that consume us and prevent living in the present moment.

I am grateful that feeling and validating my feelings helped me when my mother passed away. I reminded myself to witness, embrace, and accept my feelings without judgement. I learned to self-parent myself during the grieving process and fill the sadness and pain with acceptance, self-love, and a feeling of safety. I used deep breathing to support me to be in the present moment. As a result, when we carve out time from our hectic lives to be fully present to all our uncomfortable feelings, we liberate ourselves from the control that these feelings have over us. As time passes, we gain the ability to regulate our emotions and our responses. We feel psychologically safe and tap into the energy reserves of our empowerment battery to co-create our realities.

MENTAL DOMAIN

Coherence in the mental domain supports our ability to focus, incorporate multiple points of view, achieve clarity of thoughts, and increase our attention span so we can stay in the present moment, be true to our purpose, and share our truth using our unique voice. The mental domain consists of thought structures formed from our experiences, a lifetime of reinforcements, and deep programming of our belief systems—positive and negative—all of which start from the time we are born. Our subconscious minds are constantly being programmed by our caretakers, educational institutions, governments, entertainment channels, social media, news channels, and the environment. We absorb all the programming without judging or reasoning whether it is relevant and empowering.

Incoherence in the mental domain stems from the unconscious belief that we *are* our thoughts rather than that we *have* thoughts or are separate from our thoughts. Over time, we start to identify with the psychological and physical identity of ourselves informed by our thoughts, called the ego mind. The ego mind becomes our master, and we learn to depend on it to guide us with the constant narrative in the background informed by our history. The ego mind's job is to record and store details of all our experiences. It is an instrument of our survival to keep us safe, sane, and secure from truly feeling our feelings. It adds a false narrative to keep us within the confines of our limited comfort zone by blocking our feelings and stopping us from feeling and processing our uncomfortable feelings. Despite its benefits in helping us survive trauma when we are not capable of doing so or mature enough to learn and benefit from each experience, the mind's guidance is limited as it draws from our past experiences. Its guidance is based on the trauma and guilt of the past or the worry and anxiety of the future. While the ego mind talks to us in the present, it does not allow us to be fully in the present. It operates in the past or the future.

The ego mind's game is mental confusion. The ego mind uses many strategies and distractions to undermine our true selves and cause us to forget our true innate nature of unrivaled capacity and abilities. As a result, we are stuck in a fear and survival mode, unconsciously draining our empowerment battery and unable to create the reality we desire and deserve. The following are some of the manifestations of the ego mind.

The ego mind keeps us continually running on the treadmill of life in a state of survival, constantly seeking safety, stability, and predictability when the truth is that everything on the physical earth plane is dynamic and constantly shifting and changing (Dalconzo, 2016b). Nothing stays constant—our personal health, interpersonal relationships, careers, or finances. The ego mind prevents us from staying present in each situation or with people we interact with. At a subtler level, our nervous system has difficulty relaxing—it is either in a depressed state or a fight-or-flight state. The ego mind is our unconscious warden. The suffering we experience is our ego mind's false attempt to make us feel safe, sane, and secure by ignoring, denying, or repressing whatever we are experiencing in the present. It uses deception and creates delusions and fears to keep us safe from people and situations it perceives to be dangerous based on the trauma of past events. The ego mind uses F.E.A.R (False Evidence Appearing Real—illusion and delusion) as its energy source.

For instance, Loraine had a difficult time making lasting relationships. She felt excluded and alone in both her personal and professional life. When we worked together, she opened up and shared a childhood trauma that made her feel emotionally distant from her mom. She tried to be perfect to earn her love and felt the need to constantly prove herself to feel heard and loved. She had internalized the belief that she was not worthy of receiving love, which was reflected in her relationships. To keep her safe from experiencing her uncomfortable feeling of hurt, her ego mind created a fear-based false narrative that she had nothing of value to offer. So she distanced herself from situations and relationships.

The ego mind is a 24/7 entertainment station that never goes off the air (Dalconzo 2016b). It is addicted to excitement and instant gratification. One example of the ego mind's idea of excitement is constantly being engaged with our smartphones and computers. The ego mind enjoys drama and is either busy creating endless drama in our lives or getting us involved in someone else's drama. This depletes our energy reserves by focusing on unimportant things and staying distracted by false dramas.

The ego mind is a compulsive thinker that spends the majority of time ruminating and complaining. The ego mind is attached to how it thinks life *should be* instead of accepting life *as it is*. The ego mind is attached to a rigid plan of how our lives should unfold; it wants to control events and people. For instance, Sandra felt frustrated and angry when her family did not listen to her advice on what she felt was good for them. She felt responsible for her family. With the work we did together, she realized she had to learn to unconditionally love her family and allow them to learn from their experiences without any expectation that their actions and choices might satisfy her. She had to educate herself on boundary respect and protection.

My lesson on boundary protection was linked to my ego mind taking on a savior role. I identified as a savior for everyone. I grew up wanting to be in control of outcomes. I felt that if I controlled outcomes in all aspects of my life, I would feel safe and life would be predictable. If I did not take control, the world around me would fall apart. I unconsciously encroached on my loved ones' boundaries, taking on everyone's burdens and solving everyone's challenges. My life was one challenge after another. My actions drained me of life force energy reserves, signaling to the Universal Consciousness that I did not trust the divine growth plan. Now I learn every day to surrender to the universe's growth plan and instead use my precious energy reserves to create the fulfilling life I desire.

The ego mind believes it is entitled to be honored and adored. The quest to be honored and adored engages us in the comparison and validation game in which we are consciously or unconsciously comparing ourselves to others and seeking outside validation. This belief forces us to live within our comfort zone—living limited lives by always playing safe, not taking risks, and not making mistakes for fear of failing and "looking bad" in front of people. This belief keeps us from being our true authentic selves. We are trapped in a false persona of people-pleasing.

The ego mind engages us in the *blame, shame,* and *victim* game where we spend the majority of our time draining our empowerment battery by either blaming others or ourselves for our setbacks and adversities, feeling guilty, or becoming a victim. It provides various excuses for not taking accountability for our actions, our errors, our fears, and being in charge of our own lives. It comes up with various defenses and deflection mechanisms. Master Coach Dalconzo (1998, p. 99) states that ego defenses include "DENIAL ('it's not really happening'); REPRESSION ('it never happened'); DISSOCIATION ('I don't remember what happened'); PROJECTION ('it's happening to you, not to me'); CONVERSION ('I eat or have sex when I feel it happening'); and MINIMIZING ('it happened, but it's no big deal')." From my experience, I would add blame ("it's someone else's fault"); resistance ("I don't like what is happening—I need to be in control"); victimhood ("Poor me, why does it keep happening to me?"); guilt ("I shouldn't have done that");

superiority complex ("I am better"); and inferiority complex ("I am not good enough").

The ego mind is attached to the outcomes of actions and treats the present moment as either a means to an end or an obstacle. It seeks the next shiny accomplishment, accolade, and/or possession. It prevents us from enjoying the present moment—the beauty around us—or being fully present with people, situations, and even ourselves.

The biggest fear of the human ego mind is that we will wake up one day to the realization of its various modes of operation and how it controls us to live our lives in a constrained fear-based manner, putting up walls of resistance and defenses against situations, events, and people, trapping us in separation consciousness or a dualistic way of thinking. All these subversive strategies, although well-intentioned, subtly deplete our empowerment battery. The moment we become present to and witness the conditioned patterns of the ego mind, we stop identifying with the ego mind and its conditioned patterns. This is when the choice begins. We awaken to the discernment that our Universal-Self is the real master and that the ego mind is the servant. We begin the journey to withdraw power from our ego thoughts.

Once while meditating, I witnessed the stronghold of the obsessive nature of my ego mind. I witnessed the mechanics of how my mind nitpicked anything that it perceived was not working well and causing me frustration. It added a false narrative that contained extreme forms of negativity. When I was able to witness the phenomenon, my mind paused for a few seconds, and I experienced a glimpse of peace and tranquility.

I experienced expansion. I stopped draining my empowerment battery in my mental domain and instead chose to redirect to empowering thoughts. Witnessing helped me not spiral downward with the disempowering narrative of my thoughts. I had a profound appreciation and realization that maybe one of the unintended goals of the ego mind is to awaken me to the presence of my Universal-Self and the possibilities around me, as identifying with the ego mind leads to intense suffering. I felt grateful for this realization. I can now choose to live a fulfilling life in each moment.

To be a witness to the quality of our thoughts requires a constant, conscious effort. The quality of thoughts matters. Mahatma Gandhi summarized this principle in his writing "Guard Your Thoughts":

Keep your thoughts positive because your thoughts become your words.

Keep your words positive because your words become your behavior.

Keep your behavior positive because your behavior becomes your habits.

Keep your habits positive because your habits become your values.

Keep your values positive because your values become your destiny. (Notable Quotes)

Coherence in the mental domain liberates us from the incessant narrative and propaganda of the ego mind based on our memories of the past and uncertainty of the future. It strengthens our resolve to choose empowering thoughts in each *now* moment, stay true to our purpose, trust our abilities, and push forward despite setbacks and adversities. It strengthens our intuition and our bond with our inner guidance system. We identify with our inner guidance system and relinquish our identity with thoughts sourced from the ego mind. We come to a deep realization that we choose to be content with our lot in life and grateful for all our experiences, which are perfect for our growth and will lead us to our inner empowered selves.

The above self-realization awakens us to the innate, extraordinary power within. As we grow in confidence, we find the strength to be our authentic selves and take control of our fate. We actively co-create the life we want and deserve, and we adapt skillfully and gracefully to the difficulties life throws at us. Every day we find the courage to face our fears and make decisions that are in our best interests and for the greater good of all. We are our best ally.

Transcendence of the ego mind is challenging and requires presence. To attain coherence in the mental domain, we must train the ego mind to take a back seat and our Universal-Self to take the front seat.

Here are some tools to support coherence and resilience in the mental domain.

Witness Daily Life Triggers and Stressors

Becoming aware of the everyday triggers that often cause us to think or act in undesirable ways allows us to retrain ourselves, first by becoming a witness to the quality of our thoughts. When we become aware of the constant chatter of our ego minds as we encounter our daily stressors, we can use these triggers to reveal our unconscious negative beliefs and the operation of the ego mind. As mentioned in the emotional domain, training the feeling pathways of our brain supports us to hear what we are vocalizing and/or sub-vocalizing. Eastern philosophy calls this conscious listening being a "witness" or "observer." The power comes in the discernment between thoughts and feelings sourced from our intuitive Universal-Self versus thoughts and feelings sourced from the old, reactive, negative programming of our ego mind. During my training at the HeartMath Institute, I learned to make a list of my everyday stressors and triggers and reflect on how I react to them, their current impact, and how they deplete my energy and resilience. Once I am aware of the current impact, I can make an empowered choice to respond to the stressors. As mentioned under the spiritual domain, HeartMath Institute teaches easy-to-use, heart-based coherent techniques to connect to the intelligence of our hearts and to breathe calm and ease into the day as we encounter our stressors and triggers. A quick coherence breathing technique and other resources can be found on the HeartMath Institute website.

Witness Life Without Rose-Colored Glasses

For us to see what life reflects, we need to lower our ego defenses and see life objectively, without rose-colored glasses and without cynicism. What do our careers, finances, relationships, and health tell us about what we truly believe instead of what our ego mind is guiding us to believe (Dalconzo, 2016b)? We must reflect and learn from our patterns and beliefs what works well, what does not, and where we are relinquishing our power to that which does not serve us.

Grok That Our Inner Beliefs Create Our Outer Reality

We need to grok (internalize and emotionalize) that our inner beliefs—conscious or unconscious—create our outer reality. It is therefore necessary to identify the disempowering beliefs when they arise, do the necessary work to dis-create them, and replace them with empowering beliefs. When we realize that all our feelings of pain and pleasure depend on our mindset and how closely we are identified with our innate guidance system (our Universal-Self), we recognize that all the adversities we face are opportunities for our evolution and growth and are meant to awaken us to the power within us.

Cultivate a Focused Mindset

Incorporate presence in each task we do. Try not to rush to the completion of the tasks—whether we are having coffee or tea, cooking, eating, exercising, reading, conversing, or working. Let the task be a meditation in and of itself. In this way, we find the balance between being and doing, which means a certain aspect of us is connected to the infinite intelligence within us while we are performing the tasks. Over time and with consistent practice, the chatter of the ego mind becomes quieter, and we become more receptive to the voice of our Universal-Self. We become aware of the spaces between our thoughts. We become alert to our environment—tiny details like the smells, the sights, the sounds, the tastes. It feels as if our senses become alert and sharpened. Our intuitive sense sharpens. We expand the understanding of the beauty and the wisdom the present moment has to offer. Our lives are enriched.

Begin Each Day Connecting to the Infinite Intelligence

As mentioned under the spiritual domain, it is a healthy practice when we wake up each day—before we plunge into a barrage of emails or social media or get immersed in family responsibilities—to take at least fifteen to thirty minutes to connect to our innate guidance system through prayer or any meditative practices to find balance and harmony and to listen to the guidance we receive. It is important to pause and write down our purpose and priority list for the day. This helps set the tone of the day where we are training our minds to stay focused on what is relevant for the day. We use discernment to become agile and flexible so that we are not at the whim or fancy of the ego mind, governed by excuses and distractions, versus the guidance that is coming from our highest intelligence system. This prevents us from unnecessarily depleting our empowerment battery and supports us to wisely using our energy reserves.

Embrace Change as Constant

The ego mind resists change because of its fear of losing control, and it breeds a narrative that change is disruptive for us. We must train ourselves to see through this illusion and embrace change as a constant. We realize that we waste a lot of our energy when we resist change—when we resist life. When we learn to acknowledge, accept, let go of control, and go with the flow of what is unfolding, new possibilities and surprises emerge. It is as if we are free to enjoy the journey of life, trusting in the divine plan of our innate infinite intelligence. Nature serves as an excellent teacher of impermanence. Everything is ephemeral; there is always change. Nature does not fight back. Day is followed by night, and season is followed by season. The life cycle of creation follows the same principle that birth leads to maintenance, which leads to death.

For instance, when I was facing challenges in one of my corporate jobs, no matter what I did to improve and contribute, I was not thriving. I refused to see and accept the situation as it was. My ego mind thought that if I worked hard, I could change the situation and prove that I was valuable to the stakeholders. Six months later, when I was fired, I experienced anger, hurt, and sadness. When I went for a walk later that day to clear my head, I heard a voice that said, *This is what freedom feels like.* When I leaned into my uncomfortable feelings and thoughts, my healing journey began. Using the tools I had obtained through my coaching certification, I unearthed my unconscious negative beliefs and replaced them with empowering beliefs. I was greeted with a part-time position that allowed me to be present for nurturing my then three-year-old daughter. In addition, I started my coaching practice, healing one soul at a time—starting with my own soul. Leaning into rather than resisting change provided the needed wisdom to confront my fears and limiting beliefs and embark on a journey to trust the Universal-Self's plan for me. I learned that doubts and difficulties move us to confirm our faith and trust. St. Augustine said, "Faith is to believe what you do not see; and the reward of this faith is to see what you believe." Therefore, change needs to be embraced.

Learn and Practice Improvisation

Improvisation is a fun way to learn to get out of our comfort zone and be present to embrace and embody change. During improvisation, we learn to let go of our story narrative and be present to our partner, our surroundings, and what is unfolding in the present. We learn to go with the flow.

Many other art forms teach us the discipline of learning to be present and go with the flow. I enjoy flowing through the various yoga poses. It has taught me to go with the continuous flow and beauty of forming, maintaining, and dissolving the various poses and not getting attached to any one form.

Observe and Correct Technique

The Observe and Correct Technique promotes a growth mindset. This technique enables us to own and learn from our mistakes and make necessary changes in our behavior. We do not waste our energy making excuses for our mistakes or blaming and judging ourselves or others.

As mentioned at the beginning of this chapter, the ego mind's modus operandi to help us feel safe, sane, and secure is minimizing or denying our mistakes through our excuses. The ego mind is terrified of appearing stupid and feeling rejected and abandoned. It propagates the unconscious belief that we have to be perfect to be accepted by others and not disappoint the people we love.

The Observe and Correct Technique provides the freedom to make mistakes, take informed risks, and learn from them. We realize that life is more than playing safe in our comfort zone, controlled by our fears and the appearance of looking good. We do not rely on external validation and acceptance. We unconditionally accept ourselves and use the energy reserves from our empowerment battery to co-create the life we desire.

Practice Forgiveness

Practicing forgiveness toward ourselves and others liberates us from the continuous hurt cycle. A lack of forgiveness subtly drains huge energy reserves and keeps us trapped in emotional and mental blocks of guilt, blame, judgment, resentment, indifference, and so on. Grudges prevent us from being in the "Here Now" present moment where we can be innovative, follow our passions, and make a difference and where we can attain and live with our full potential.

Jennifer was not ready to forgive the people who had hurt her. I explained to her how holding on to anger leads to the depletion of her energy, leaving her without energy reserves to create her reality. I shared with her the "potato exercise" that I learned during my coaching certification. She purchased a sack of potatoes and wrote down the name of one person who hurt her on one potato each, then put them all in the sack. For an entire week, she carried this sack everywhere she went, including meetings, driving to her appointments, meeting her clients, going grocery shopping, and eating at restaurants. As you can imagine, not only was the bag heavy, but the condition of the potatoes deteriorated over time. She had a wake-up call about how carrying unforgiveness was harming her. The sack of potatoes is a metaphor for the emotional baggage we carry when we believe in the narrative the ego mind propagates, stagnating and deteriorating us on the inside and making us susceptible to illness and diseases. It prevents us from being present to the abundance and beauty around us.

Forgiveness does not mean we have to condone the dysfunctional behaviors of others who have hurt us. We surrender to the higher intelligence for divine justice to free us from the vicious cycle of negativity. Forgiveness is a self-protection mechanism. Forgiveness allows us to refuse to accept the toxic influence of our past so we can dispense our energy to create what we desire.

We learn to forgive ourselves for our dysfunctional behaviors so that we do not remain trapped in the guilt emotion that not only makes us feel unworthy but also drains our vital energy reserves. We learn from our dysfunctional behaviors so that we do not keep repeating them over again.

Practice Boundary Protection

We learned boundary literacy under the spiritual domain. Mature boundaries are a hallmark of healthy relationships with ourselves and others. A lack of boundary literacy leads us to use childlike ego defenses to defend ourselves (Dalconzo 2016b, p. 39). We need to learn how to maturely protect our boundaries with the right person, in the right manner, to the right degree, and in the right way (Dalconzo, 2016b, p. 39). Some boundary protection techniques to consider include not taking things personally, saying no and yes strategically, and respecting ourselves.

The *ability to not take things personally* (Ruiz, 1997) grows over time as we learn to identify with our infinite Universal-Self and when we internalize and emotionalize that we are unique manifestations of the Universal Consciousness. This recognition helps us realize that we are in charge of our behavior and choices and should not become attached to those of others. We learn to respect boundaries. We learn to believe and trust in our uniqueness, talents, and abilities. We have opportunities to learn and grow. We view feedback as opportunities to learn. For instance, during one of the meetings I was facilitating, a team member lost his cool when he felt he was held responsible for the delay in the program. This resulted in a chaotic meeting. I retained my calm and explained what I meant when I reviewed the timelines at the meeting. As a follow-up, we agreed to have frequent communication to keep each other updated on the progress of the program. Instead of getting caught in an emotional outburst, I decided to focus on what was important for the program and the greater good of the team.

Saying no to your no and yes to your yes is another key boundary-setting skill. Having clarity about our boundaries builds an internal compass for our authentic selves. It teaches us not to lower our moral standards to be accepted. It promotes a healthy self-image. When we learn to be honest with ourselves, we are more likely to be honest with everyone around us. Shakespeare's Hamlet captures this principle when Polonius, the chief minister of King Claudius, counsels his son, Laertes, on how to act while attending university. He advises his son, "This above all: To thine own self be true, and it must follow, as the night the day, thou canst not then be false to any man."

Respecting ourselves is another key skill for maintaining healthy boundaries. Respecting ourselves helps us be in the present moment and witness the narrative of our minds. When I am hard on myself and when I subconsciously identify with negative intrusive thoughts, I pause to listen and recognize that the narrative is coming from my ego mind. I remind myself to be loving and kind to myself first. Being loving and kind to myself allows me to extend the same grace to family, clients, and coworkers. I can only give what I have. This programs our nervous system that we are worthy of being addressed in a kind, empowering, and compassionate way and that we are unique manifestations of divine innate intelligence. Keeping our word to ourselves is empowering. It signals that we possess self-esteem and self-love and are committed to ourselves. We are our best ally. We first have to learn to respect ourselves before we respect others.

Cultivate an Attitude of Gratitude

Reflecting and listing each day the things we are grateful for cultivates an awareness within us of all that is going well in our lives, and that we are abundantly blessed with. A grateful heart views challenges as opportunities for growth and stepping out of our comfort zones. This builds a deep trust that all our experiences serve a purpose for our growth and that our inner guidance system is always working in our favor. There are no good or bad experiences—only a stream of experiences for us to be present to what we are experiencing at any given moment. This builds curiosity to lean into our experiences and fully embrace and gain wisdom from our experiences. It builds our capacity for inner resilience to respond to life challenges gracefully and to co-create the reality we desire in partnership with our guidance system.

At the dinner table with my family each day, we go around to share what we are grateful for about the day and about each other. This gratitude practice anchors us to pause and appreciate the abundance of the present moment and the uniqueness of each other. It fosters psychological safety within us as we are in tune with the beauty around us and within us.

Witness Resistance

Witnessing resistance requires being present and acknowledging our ego defenses on where and how we are resisting life. It is, in essence, the same tool as witnessing life without rose-colored glasses, where we are brutally honest with ourselves and evaluate each pillar of our life—personal, relationships, finances, careers—wherever or in whatever way we are resisting life. It requires us to witness the narrative of our ego mind in each pillar to examine where we are holding on to situations, people, and objects and where we are giving our power away. As mentioned at the beginning of the chapter, I was resisting life by stepping in and taking on a savior role, identifying as a savior for everyone to feel safe. I refused to accept the situations for what they were and unconsciously felt I needed to step in to take control and help out. I unconsciously tied my self-worth to how best I could assist. This impacted my relationships as I unconsciously encroached on my loved ones' boundaries, taking on everyone's burdens and solving everyone's challenges. I unconsciously lacked a deep trust in the universe's growth plan for each individual. I was unaware that each individual is born with a guidance system that is constantly guiding them. I am learning to witness where I am resisting situations or people and instead take time to accept the situations as they unfold and learn to respond based on the guidance from my Universal-Self. The poem "Resistance" captures the essence of non-resistance, acceptance, and presence in each moment of our life experiences. Resistance bears a wealth of information that needs to be deciphered and understood. Once understood and assimilated, we embody the power to consciously stop draining our empowerment battery.

"Resistance"
(Dalconzo 1998, p. 110)
When I resist "what is"
I'm resisting what I co-created,
I'm resisting what I need to learn,
I'm resisting what I need to heal.
I'm resisting . . . the "I Am" of me!
Resistance needs to be embraced . . .
Resistance needs to be explored . . .
Resistance needs to be understood.
Resistance shows me where my ego
is clinging to my past,
or yearning for my future,
which disengages me from the Now!
Resistance needs to be accepted . . .
Resistance needs to be released . . .
Resistance needs to be transcended.
Resistance is my ego.. . . .
trying to make "what is" into what I "think" it should be!
Resistance is my ego . . . trying to make me feel safe,
by attempting to control "what is!"
When I resist any element of my life,
I'm fighting against the flow of the whole Universe!
When I surrender to "what is"
I see the truth, I'm in the flow,
and I go merrily down
the stream of Life.

PHYSICAL DOMAIN

The physical domain is the action domain. This is where the rubber of life hits the road. Coherence and resilience in the physical domain provide us with the strength and endurance to fully integrate and embody the wisdom and coherence of the spiritual, emotional, and mental domains in our physical body through action. This enables us to show up empowered to not only respond to the challenges of the day but also to utilize our energy to co-create the reality and miracles we are here to create based on our purpose and passion.

    Recurrent practices for building coherence in the spiritual, emotional, and mental domains create psychological safety and peace in our bodies. We feel safe and at home in our bodies. We emit joy. We have an air of lightness and playfulness in us. I noticed a subtle shift in my relationship with my daughter as I created psychological safety in my body. I was more relaxed, and she sensed it. She connected to the inner playful child inside me, and we were able to bond deeply together. I was able to be freed from my rigid structure reins of what I felt were nurturing and supporting her and instead learn to enjoy the present moment with her.

Coherence in the physical domain empowers us to take action to realize our full potential as we come to the realization and acceptance that we are co-creators of our reality. We create our realities based on the frequencies we are vibrating. As mentioned under the spiritual domain, we each have an energy signature that is unique in the whole universe—our unique combination of electrons and photons. The universe manifests what we are a vibrational match to. Because like attracts like, when we emit high, happy, and positive vibrations, we attract people and experiences into our lives that foster inspiration, opportunity, and expansion. On the other hand, when we emit worry, fear, self-doubt, anxiety, and anger, we attract experiences and people that match those negative vibrations. We realize that the underlying essence and mechanism for the manifestation of our reality are linked to our vibrational frequency, which is intricately linked to our beliefs and thoughts. When our beliefs and thoughts are empowering, we vibrate at a higher frequency and show up in the world as loving, peaceful instruments of light, making a difference by being our authentic selves, through our thoughts, words, and actions. At the quantum level, we input love, joy, and positivity into the world. In contrast, when our beliefs are disempowering, we identify and align our vibrational frequency with the limiting programmed patterns of our ego mind—we vibrate at a lower frequency and show up as fear-based, inauthentic individuals who are pretending to be someone we are not and living a limited, fear-based life of perpetual survival. At the quantum level, we unconsciously input fear, lack, anger, conflict, turmoil, trauma, worry, and suffering into the world. Therefore, being aware of the actions and vibrations linked to the beliefs and thoughts we are sending out into the universe serves an important purpose for us and the world.

We experience the consequences of our actions. According to Dalconzo, "Every action generates a force of energy that returns to me in kind; therefore, what I sow, I reap! When we choose actions that are open, honest, and spiritually centered, the fruits of our actions will attract the same. If our thoughts resonate with fear and our actions are riddled with pain, fear, and mistrust, the fruits of our actions will mirror our fear-based actions!" (1998, p. 217). When we show love and compassion to others, we experience a hundred times more of it ourselves. When we spread hate, fear, resentment, or manipulation, we receive the same emotions a hundred times in return. The consequences of our actions provide us with an opportunity to learn, grow, and be empowered by them. It is saying yes to creating affirming life experiences and adventures.

To manifest what we want to co-create, we need to be clear about our intentions and the objectives we choose to create, and we take inspired actions. If we cannot define what we want, we can't have it. For the universe to make our desires come true, it receives our intentions as quantum information, which then triggers the infinite organizing power of our Universal-Self. It is comparable to putting a precise location marker on Google Maps. We deserve to co-create the experiences we desire and to live our lives the way we want them to be.

Our word becomes the law within the universe. We signal to the universe that we are sincere through our actions. Without action, the intention has no significance and no meaning. Without action, there is stagnation in all four domains—physical, emotional, mental, and spiritual.

In addition, coherence in the physical domain provides us with the resolve to live our most authentic lives doing what we are passionate about and what sets our souls on fire. We are true to our unique calling in life—our unique purpose for our life on earth. It pushes us out of bed each day to answer the call, rain or shine. Our actions have clarity of purpose. We do not look for acceptance or approval from others. External acknowledgments and accolades have limited value. Our life has meaning and value without outside endorsement. We operate from our fully charged inner empowerment battery, harnessing the power of our unique talents and gifts. We vibrate at a higher frequency and attract our intentions and desires. We effortlessly create solutions to any obstacles we face. We feel joyful and uplifted, which reverberates through our voices and our bodies. When we look back on life, there are no regrets. We do not die with a song in our hearts, and we are like a bird that sings at the break of dawn. When we are not living our life's purpose and when we are working jobs that are meaningless to us, our life seems like a drag. We are operating at our suboptimal power as our inner empowerment battery drains. We vibrate at a lower frequency and experience difficulty attracting and manifesting our heart's desires. This depletes our life force energy as we are not fully present to enjoy life. Even minor road bumps seem like huge mountains to cross. As the popular saying goes, "When you do the work you love, you'll never have to work another day in your life!" We create and enjoy the experiences of financial freedom.

Let's discuss some key tools to support coherence and resilience in the physical domain. These include mastering the conscious co-creation process, replenishing our inner empowerment battery, always doing our best, learning from our experiences, and taking responsibility for our actions.

Study, Practice, Internalize, and Emotionalize the Conscious Co-Creation Process

The conscious co-creation process has three steps. Studying, practicing, internalizing, and emotionalizing the three steps builds new neural pathways for manifesting our reality.

Step 1: Dis-Creation

In this step, we deprogram the dysfunctional belief and reprogram the functional belief. The first step of dis-creation involves the awareness and deprogramming of ingrained, reactive, unconscious, dysfunctional beliefs, thoughts, and behaviors that are no longer useful for our growth; the second step involves the reprogramming and re-creation of empowering beliefs that support stepping out of our comfort zone and creating the reality we desire and deserve. One of the secrets of creating empowering beliefs is to emotionalize with passion positive affirmations for the manifestation of our desires. Emotionalizing with passion is what ignites the electromagnetic energy needed to help us create new belief systems (Dalconzo, 2017). Dr. Joe Dispenza, in a YouTube TEDx Tacoma video (2013), explains that emotionalizing with passion causes nerve cells in the brain to activate and fuse together to create new neural pathways. The more times a particular thought is repeated with passion and feeling, the stronger and deeper the neural pathway becomes. Consistent and repetitious thoughts give rise to beliefs that influence our behavior. Conversely, if we stop stimulating neural pathways that are anchored to negative thoughts, eventually those connections will dissolve and dis-create the negative thoughts. This requires us to be a witness to the quality of our thoughts in each "now moment," as mentioned in the mental domain. Witnessing the quality of our thoughts empowers us to withdraw power from our disempowering thoughts and replace them with empowering thoughts.

Step 2: Set Clear Intentions and Objectives

Taking the time to visualize, laying out the details, and writing down the things we want to create, what we are passionate about, and the reasons behind them supports us in being clear about our intentions, desires, and objectives. Daring to dream big and setting no limits on our imagination is a powerful tool of creation.

Step 3: Take Action and Trust in Our Unique Abilities

Each day, we focus and take empowering steps, no matter how small, toward our intention. Each day, we connect and listen to the intuitive Universal-Self through meditation and stillness. Then we take action. Nothing happens until we act. Note that "faith without action creates confusion and delusion and serves no useful purpose" (Dalconzo 2016a, p. 58). Action demonstrates the courage we need to take charge of our lives and row our lifeboats. It is fully trusting that our Universal-Self is orchestrating events for the manifestation of our desires. To fulfill our intentions, we are required to focus our attention on the present and do our best each day. Giving voice to our intentions and passions reminds us of our uniqueness, inspires us, and boosts our self-esteem and our self-confidence. It keeps us grounded, staying in our power instead of looking outside ourselves, comparing ourselves to others, and getting trapped in the "less than" narrative of the ego mind. We become more courageous and assertive when we are living our authentic selves.

Cultivating discipline to create a plan of action and ensuring the completion of tasks provides the fuel and energy required to keep our passions alive. It keeps us anchored to our purpose and teaches us to value and use time to our advantage. It boosts our self-confidence and self-esteem.

When we see and feel how our actions impact us and everybody around us, we stay connected to our passions and our unique gifts. We see and feel the difference between living our purpose versus chasing after external illusions and instant gratifications. We are likely to stay connected to our purpose, as it fills us with joy and peace that no external force can fill. We unwittingly inspire others around us to live their authentic purpose.

We understand that struggle is part of the process. We are more likely to persist in the face of challenges or setbacks when we learn that struggle is a natural part of life. Life is a patient instructor. We must venture forth into the world and encounter what we came here to encounter. Challenges are necessary for our growth and character building. They keep us going when the going gets tough. Thomas Edison eloquently stated, "I have not failed. I've just found 10,000 ways that won't work." We trust in our abilities. Life is a learning experience. Creating experiences, learning, and growing from them are more important than acquiring and regurgitating knowledge. Taking informed risks, creating, learning, and failing will build a more fulfilling life than leading a passive life with little or no failures. Being afraid to act because of the fear of failure leads to a disempowered life. Sometimes lurking behind the fear of failure lies the unconscious belief that we must please others and not let them down, or that we must always look good. "Fail" stands for "First Attempt in Learning" (F.A.I.L.), and the goal in our life is to learn and evolve and not be limited to pleasing others and looking good.

List the Energy Activities That Replenish Your Inner Empowerment Battery

Tune in to what makes your cup full. Even if we take one action that fills our cup each day, it fills us with the energy and strength we need to take care of our responsibilities. We possess a playful attitude and ease toward our responsibilities. I have incorporated the following recurrent practices into my lifestyle. This is not an all-inclusive list. Please take what resonates and add what replenishes you to the list (Johnson, 2023).

- **Prayer and Meditation:** When I pray, I take the time to connect and communicate with the life force energy of my Universal-Self. This is my time to communicate with my Universal-Self about what I am experiencing, how I am feeling, and what I want to manifest. I seek guidance on how to navigate challenges and predicaments. I give thanks for my loved ones, my experiences, and all the resources I am blessed with because I live on this beautiful planet. In meditation, I sit in stillness to connect with and listen to the intuitive messages from my Universal-Self. At times, I receive guidance as to what steps to take to solve my predicaments or co-create what I desire.

- **Visualization:** I take time to visualize in detail, feel, and write down the things I want to create and the reasons behind them. I lay out every detail and give my Universal-Self complete control to direct how it will manifest. I feel empowered as I co-create with my Universal-Self.

- **Nature baths:** I enjoy immersing myself in nature by taking walks or jogs, going on hikes, being mindful of the world around me, or gazing up at various cloud formations. I am able to pause the compulsive thoughts of my ego mind to enjoy the present moment and to create a feeling of expansiveness within.

- **Yoga:** Yoga empowers me because it not only helps to stretch my body but also calms the busy chatter in my mind. I feel good, refreshed, and nimble after taking a yoga class or practicing yoga stretches in the comforts of my home.

- **Nutrition.** I take satisfaction in planning and preparing delicious, high-energy meals for my family and myself. I often cut vegetables for the week, making it simple to include them in meals when I am pressed for time.

- **Sleep.** Before retiring to bed, I turn off all my electronics, take a warm bath, drink a warm cup of decaffeinated tea, and spend five to ten minutes in prayer and meditation. For me, six to seven hours of undisturbed, restorative sleep is enough to feel renewed.

- **Heart coherent breathing techniques.** I practice HeartMath Institute's coherent breathing techniques to regulate my emotions and increase my energy reserves (empowerment capacity). These techniques are heart-centered, simple, and portable, allowing me to practice them while I drive, shop, or take a quick stroll around the block. Bringing my attention back to my heart and taking slow, deep breaths enables me to disconnect for a few moments from the business of my mind and intentionally connect with my Universal-Self. It anchors me to breathe calm and ease into my day.

- **Energy drills.** I express thanks in advance and restate my positive affirmations with electromagnetic intensity so that my words reverberate into the universe, and I feel as though my desires have already materialized and are on their way to me.

- **Quality time.** My vibrations and joy rise when I spend quality time being present, laughing, and playing with family, friends, and our kitten.

- **Comedy movies.** I enjoy laughing aloud while watching comedies. I find it beneficial to raise my vibrational frequency and not take life too seriously.

Do Our Best, Always

Ninety-nine percent of life is showing up and doing our best each day without getting attached to outcomes. Giving our best effort and not obsessing about so-called "results" encourages a growth mindset. We are liberated from the constraints of the ego mind that is fixated on outcomes and prevents us from experiencing the moment. We learn to appreciate and understand the journey of creation. We experience the joy of living a life of faith in deeds and learn to trust and believe in our Universal-Self. We appreciate all that we have and do not take anything for granted. We appreciate the accolades and accomplishments we achieved, but we learn not to let them define who we are. We realize life is a journey and not a destination. We learn there are no shortcuts in life. We need to be fully present with the adventures and teachings that each phase of the journey has to offer. We put our essence and passion into the journey. The present moment is all we have, and we learn to cherish it. We learn to go with the flow.

Learn from Our Experiences

We learn to be grateful for our experiences, no matter how painful, as they provide an opportunity to grow, step outside our comfort zone, and transform ourselves. It requires the courage of a hero to lean into our experiences, witness our unconscious or conscious behaviors, and ask the question, "What can I learn and how can I grow from this experience?" Healing and transformation happen when we awaken to the realization that there is no value in attaching to and identifying with past pain and suffering. The ego mind basks in familiarity and power when we identify with our past hurts and live a life of victimhood, guilt, and shame. Experiences awaken us to the limitless power within us.

Take Responsibility for Our Actions

When we take responsibility for our actions, we learn to accept the consequences of our behaviors without any resentment, negativity, or blame. We do not become trapped in the blame, shame, and victim game. We wake up to the empowering realization that we are the cause of our reality, and if we do not like the reality we are in, we possess the power within us to dis-create it and co-create another reality. We cultivate a growth mindset. We feel energized as we have energy reserves to be present and say yes to life each day, each moment.

PART I SUMMARY

The key to coherent communication is being an ally to oneself first before we can be an ally to others. We are born with an inner empowerment battery—our inner guidance system that is all-knowing, all-loving, infinite, compassionate, and all-truth. When we take the time to connect with our inner guidance system through coherence in each of our four interrelated domains, we feel the infinite love, wisdom, intelligence, and compassion of our guidance system, and we feel psychologically safe. We feel psychologically safe in our bodies as our hearts, emotions, thoughts, hormonal and autonomous nervous systems, and actions are in sync. We are not in a fight-or-flight mode. At the spiritual level, we are our unique, peaceful, authentic selves living our purpose each day and tolerant of others' values and beliefs; at the emotional level, we possess the maturity to regulate our emotions and maintain a positive outlook; at the mental level, we have empowering thoughts and behaviors; and at the physical level, we have healthy, vibrant bodies, we are wise in our actions, and we are co-creators of our reality. We operate from our fully charged inner empowerment battery. We are our own strongest ally. We communicate with our coherent hearts, and we are fully present in our communication and interactions. By being our strongest ally, we are allies to others. We realize at a deeper level that we are all connected through our inner guidance system—our Universal-Self. We offer the same sense of psychological safety to others wherever we go.

It is our responsibility through consistent nurturing practices in each of our four domains to connect, identify, and build unrelenting trust with our inner guidance system. As mentioned at the beginning of Part I, the fundamental truth that pervades and ties the performance of all four domains is that our underlying beliefs—conscious or unconscious—create our reality. Our subconscious minds are constantly being programmed by our caretakers, our educational systems, our governments, our work institutions, our environment, and social media. We absorb the programming without assessing whether it is empowering and relevant for us. The biggest unconscious negative belief we are raised to believe, passed down through endless generations of fear-based programming, is that we are separate from our inner guidance system and from each other. Therefore, it is our responsibility to unearth the limiting beliefs that separate us from our inner guidance system and limit us from reaching our full potential by subtly draining our empowerment battery.

Spiritual Domain

When we identify and build a trusting relationship with our inner guidance system, we realize we are never alone, and we are safe in the light of our inner guidance system. We each are unique manifestations of our Universal-Self, with our unique energy signature, features, abilities, talents, and strengths. When we embrace and love our uniqueness, we learn to accept ourselves with all our imperfections and perfections. We learn to separate ourselves from our behaviors. We lean into our experiences, witness our dysfunctional behaviors, and ask ourselves what we can learn and how we can grow from each experience. We take ownership of our dysfunctional behaviors and do not make any excuses.

Mastering the fundamental truths of the spiritual domain provides us the clarity of our purpose in life and the values governing our lives. We learn and respect our boundaries and are not enmeshed in other's fear-based belief systems and values. We possess the needed self-esteem and self-confidence to recognize our self-worth. We show up each day as our authentic selves living our purpose. We live with an urgency each day regarding what our legacy will be, knowing our time on this planet is limited. We do not take life for granted. We take time each day to connect to our inner guidance system through prayer, meditation, practicing heart coherent techniques, being present to enjoy the beauty around us, and connecting to our creative sides.

Emotional Domain

The emotional domain is where we unearth limiting beliefs that separate us from our Universal-Self through our feelings. Our feelings are the gateway to receiving intuitive messages when we are in alignment with our Universal-Self and when we are out of alignment with our Universal-Self. When we are taught to think and rationalize our feelings, rather than "to feel" our feelings, the feelings stay in our bodies as blocked emotions forming neural pathways that do not serve us well, triggering the stress hormone cortisol, which impacts our metabolism, sleep patterns, and immune system, drains our empowerment battery, and leads to diseases.

Coherence in our emotional domain is achieved by learning the language of feelings. When we sit in stillness, we allow ourselves to feel all the comfortable and uncomfortable feelings in our bodies, and we acknowledge and own our feelings without judgment. We awaken to the hidden wisdom behind them. They reveal patterns of our dysfunctional behaviors and our unconscious negative beliefs. We are no longer hijacked by our unprocessed feelings running our lives. Instead, we are empowered to regulate our emotions, leading to empowered choices for our challenges. We stop depleting our empowerment battery through our blocked emotions and instead use our energy to co-create what we desire.

Mental Domain

Coherence in the mental domain is realized when we awaken to the discernment that our Universal-Self is our internal North Star—our real master guiding us to be the best version of ourselves—and that the ego mind is our servant. When we awaken to this discernment, we understand and witness the workings of the ego mind. We understand that the ego mind keeps us safe and confines us in the safety of our comfort zone, where we continuously seek stability and predictability as we run on the treadmill of life. It creates delusions and is attached to a rigid plan of how our lives should unfold and what outcomes should come about, using the present moment as a means to an end. The ego mind governs us by a continuous stream of thoughts informed by the trauma and guilt of the past, or the worry and anxiety of the future, without being in the present moment. It engages in excuses, blame, shame, and the victim game to avoid accountability and taking responsibility. The ego mind is a 24/7 entertainment channel that traps us with the distractions of social media, instant gratification, and the creation of endless dramas in our own and other's lives. It seeks external validation and approval, believing it is entitled to be honored and adored.

Once we understand the modes of operation of the ego mind, we begin to step back to witness the quality of our thoughts. We take steps to withdraw the power from our limiting ego thoughts and replace them with empowering thoughts. We unearth powerful unconscious negative beliefs related to the limiting thoughts that drain our empowerment battery and prevent us from identifying with our Universal-Self. The fundamental truth is that we are separate from our thoughts.

When we take the time to study, practice, internalize, and emotionalize the truth that we are separate from our thoughts, we gain deep wisdom from all our life experiences through reflection and introspection. We are no longer trapped in the web of confining ego thoughts. We discern the thoughts that are sourced from our intuitive Universal-Self and thoughts that are sourced from the ego mind. We begin to build coherence in our mental domain when we internalize that our beliefs (conscious and unconscious) create our reality. We witness the daily life stressors and triggers in our lives that guide us to unconscious limiting negative beliefs that govern the functioning of the ego mind. We garner the courage to witness our life without rose-colored glasses so that we can clearly view in what pillar of our life we are facing challenges and unknowingly giving our power away: our personal lives, our careers, our relationships, our finances, and/or our health.

We educate ourselves on mental boundary protection. We do not take things personally as we know and identify with our Universal-Self and trust in our uniqueness, talents, and abilities. We are clear about our values and possess a healthy self-image. We do not compromise our values and do not create or get enmeshed in others' dramas. We respect ourselves and honor our commitment to ourselves. We observe, own, and correct our dysfunctional behaviors instead of being caught in a blame, shame, or victim game reactive cycle. We practice forgiveness toward ourselves and others as we realize that divine justice is the best justice, and we have the choice to learn and grow from our mistakes.

We cultivate an attitude of gratitude for all our experiences, as we realize that all our experiences are orchestrated to awaken us to the divinity within and to reclaim our power. Our Universal-Self pervades each experience, and we are actors playing various roles on the stage of life. Our experiences are teachers in disguise, guiding us on our path to union with our Universal-Self. We detach from the outcomes and expectations of our experiences and learn to go with the flow. We embrace change as constant. We cultivate a focused mindset, being fully present with what and how we are doing.

Physical Domain

The physical domain is the action domain where we apply and embody the wisdom and unconditional love of the coherence of our spiritual, emotional, and mental domains in our physical bodies. Coherence in the physical domain means that our nervous system is not in a fight-or-flight mode. Our nervous system, our hormonal system, our hearts, and our minds are in sync. We feel secure in being our authentic selves and living our purpose each day with courage and grace. We have embodied the wisdom that there is only one of us in the universe vibrating with our unique energy signature—our own combination of electrons and photons. We attract experiences based on our vibrational frequency. Our vibrational frequency is intricately linked to our beliefs and our thoughts. When our beliefs and our thoughts are empowering, we show up in the world as loving, peaceful instruments making a difference through our thoughts, words, and actions. We align our vibrational frequency with our Universal-Self. At the quantum level, we input love and positivity into the world.

Our actions matter. We understand that there are consequences to our actions, and we reap what we sow. When we choose actions that are honest, open, and spiritually centered, the fruits of action attract the same manyfold. On the other hand, when our actions spread hate, resentment, fear, or manipulation, we experience the same manyfold. Healing and transformation from our actions happen when we embrace the opportunity and the responsibility to learn from the consequences of our actions. We ask ourselves, "What can I learn and how can I grow from this experience?" We view our experiences as stepping stones rather than obstacles. When we feel empowered, we say yes to life adventures and experiences as we realize that we are the co-creators of our reality in partnership with our Universal-Self. Ninety-nine percent of life is showing up each day and taking actions based on our inner guidance system.

It is our responsibility to keep the vibrational energy of our bodies high by listing and routinely doing energy-replenishing activities that replenish our inner empowerment battery and fill our cups. When our vibrations are at a higher frequency, we are co-creators of our reality. We have focused objectives and clear intentions about what we want to co-create. We understand and apply the three steps of the conscious co-creation process.

The first step is to dis-create any reactive, ingrained, dysfunctional beliefs, thoughts, and behaviors that are not empowering and useful for our growth and development. We reprogram our nervous system with empowering beliefs. One of the secrets to embodying and reprograming our nervous system with empowering beliefs is to emotionalize with passion positive affirmations for the manifestation of our desires. Emotionalizing with passion reverberates the positive affirmations through our body, creating deep neural pathways and giving rise to empowering beliefs that influence our behaviors.

The second step of the conscious co-creation process is that we set clear intentions and objectives about what we want. Being clear and laying down the details of what we want and why we want it provides the energy and clarity required for conscious co-creation.

We next take actions based on our inner guidance system by connecting to our Universal-Self and listening each day through meditation and prayer. We cultivate the discipline to create a plan of action and follow through by ensuring the completion of tasks. We understand that struggle and failure are part of the creation process, and necessary for our growth and character building. This fosters a growth mindset.

Therefore, taking the time each day to build coherence in each of our four interrelated domains through recurrent practices builds a strong identification, deep connection, and trust with our inner guidance system. We feel psychologically safe and peaceful in our hearts, emotions, thoughts, minds, and bodies. We respond to challenges and adversities with grace, and we co-create the reality we desire with courage and a single-pointed focus. We are our strongest ally. We are coherent and empowered in our communication. As I work each day on embodying coherence, I notice a subtle feeling of psychological safety and an awareness of abundance and blessings all around me that I was unaware of before.

PART II

As a little girl growing up in India, I was drawn to the poem "Abou Ben Adhem" by Leigh Hunt:

> Abou Ben Adhem (may his tribe increase!)
> Awoke one night from a deep dream of peace,
> And saw, within the moonlight in his room,
> Making it rich, and like a lily in bloom,
> An angel writing in a book of gold:—
> Exceeding peace had made Ben Adhem bold,
> And to the presence in the room he said,
> "What writest thou?"—The vision rais'd its head,
> And with a look made of all sweet accord,
> Answer'd, "The names of those who love the Lord,"
> "And is mine one?" said Abou. "Nay, not so,"
> Replied the angel. Abou spoke more low,
> But cheerly still, and said, "I pray thee then,
> Write me as one that loves his fellow-men!"

> The angel wrote, and vanish'd. The next day
> It came again with a great wakening light,
> And show'd the names whom love of God had bless'd,
> And lo! Ben Adhem's name led all the rest.

On reflection, this poem resonates deeply as it highlights self-allyship. Abou Ben Adhem had attained deep peace within—psychological safety. He was his authentic self. He did not panic when the angel told him that his name was not on the list of those who love God. Instead, he requested to be on the list of those who love their fellowmen. The poem is beautiful and powerful, as it conveys the message that profound blessings await us when we are at peace with who we are and when we are an ally to others.

Part II explores techniques of coherent communication on how to be an ally to others. As stated in Part I, we can only give others what we already possess. When we are allies to ourselves first, our natural response is to be allies to others. With our cups full and flowing, we show up being the better version of ourselves and supporting others. We understand what it means in practice to put our oxygen masks on first before helping others. We understand the essence and application of the Golden Rule to treat others the way you want to be treated. My favorite Maya Angelou quote has always been "I've learned that people will forget what you said, people will forget what you did, but people will never forget how you made them feel" (Kaiser, 2016).

When we are allies to ourselves, we view conflict, crisis, change, and communication with difficult people through a different lens—not a lens of separation but a lens of curiosity, discovery, and exploration based on the fundamental truth that the universal wisdom dwells within us and others. We are not separate from each other. We are connected to each other through our all-knowing, all-powerful, all-loving, all-compassionate, and peaceful inner guidance system. At a deeper level, we realize that solutions to challenges and adversities exist when we take the time to sit in stillness, connect to our guidance system, and ask the questions "What wisdom is this challenge or conflict showing me? How is this challenge serving me? What is the solution for this challenge or conflict that results in the mutual benefit for all involved?" We will be surprised at what wisdom and solutions emerge.

When we are at peace with who we are and have the courage to shine our inner light, we model and inspire others to shine their light. We let go of our need to control others or depend on others for our happiness. We are the change we desire to see in others. In addition, we have the realization that not everyone will be aware of the presence of their inner guidance system on how to be an ally to themselves, and therefore their behaviors will be governed by the conditioned patterns of their ego mind.

I once overheard a conversation in the lunchroom at work about the protests supporting the ceasefire in Gaza. One person was asking another, "How can protests in the United States stop the long-standing conflict in Gaza between Palestine and Israel?" On deeper reflection, I thought, when we have assimilated the fundamental truths, we are all connected through the infinite intelligence, love, and compassion of our inner guidance system, we are unique manifestations of the infinite intelligence system, and we all share the same destiny that our time on this planet is limited. We then wake up to the realization that the quality of our actions matters. We have the courage to stand up for truth, as at the quantum level we are all interconnected. We make a difference through the quality of our actions. Through the recurrent embodiment of coherent practices in each of the four interrelated domains, we deepen our trust in our inner guidance system.

One of the hidden truths in being allies to others is that it helps us to surface and heal areas of ourselves where we are governed by our fears and limiting beliefs and inadvertently giving our power away. During the 2024 election year, while checking out at the grocery store, I thanked the cashier and wished her "Happy Holidays." She replied that she wasn't sure the holidays were going to be happy given that the politicians were running the country to the ground. I told her that she has the power to vote, pray, and volunteer for causes she was passionate about. She sounded doubtful that any of the suggestions would help. As I was driving home back, I got a sense that she was giving her power to despair. I reflected on areas of my life where I was giving my power away through self-doubts, not speaking up for myself, not stepping out of my comfort zone, and so on. There is a blessing in being an ally to others, as it creates awareness to be an ally to ourselves.

Below are some of the techniques I have found effective for being an ally to others through my learning, growth, and experiences. These techniques weave a beautiful tapestry using psychological safety and trust, empowering us to live

PART II

in harmony with one another despite our differences and work together to build a flourishing society. Please add to the list the techniques that work best for you, as I believe there are abundant solutions for an open heart with a pure intention to create solutions that benefit and uplift all of humanity.

TEN TECHNIQUES TO BECOME AN ALLY TO OTHERS

1. Have a Clear Purpose and Desired Outcome

I have come across multiple situations in my personal and professional life when interactions with people do not have a clear purpose and desired outcome. This may result in reacting with conditioned patterns of the ego mind. I catch myself when I get into an argument or disagreement with my loved ones or coworkers, sometimes not realizing why I got into the argument in the first place and being swept by my emotions. When the ego mind and emotions dominate communication and interaction, it is a fertile ground for chaos, confusion, drama, misunderstandings, and conflict. In his book *The Power of Now*, Eckhart Tolle says that the "mind-identified state is severely dysfunctional" (1997, p. 188), that we are compelled to think, feel, and act in particular ways according to the programming of our ego mind. Nobody chooses dysfunction, insanity, conflict, or suffering. Due to a lack of conscious awareness and presence in us, the past darkness remains (p. 188). When our responses result from identification with the ego mind, we may unconsciously create more suffering for ourselves, our loved ones, our coworkers, and all we interact with around us.

Therefore, having a clear purpose, keeping a bigger picture in mind, and listening with a coherent heart helps us course-correct when conversations go awry. We are not preoccupied with the constant chatter of the ego mind in the background or distracted by social media. We keep our composure, are clear about our purpose, and listen with an open heart and mind. We are psychologically safe as we are committed to the practice of being an ally to ourselves first. We are anchored to our purpose. This enables us to have heart-to-heart interactions, be present for the other person to feel heard and seen, align on creative solutions for the challenge at hand, and spend quality time together. I apply this technique when setting clear agendas for meetings with a clear purpose and desired outcome for the topic under discussion. This provides an anchor when the conversations go in different directions, and it helps bring the conversation back to what the team is working on accomplishing now, at the present moment.

At work, this technique offered me a new perspective when I was tasked, along with a team, to recommend solutions to reduce the "number of meetings" in the company. When I shared my ideas, one of the team members dismissed my ideas, stating that his ideas were better suited to solving the challenge. I assertively reminded him that each of us has our own unique set of ideas and that he was free to share his ideas and/or expand on those that I had suggested. It dawned on me that night that we all have a distinct set of experiences and are excited to use them to tackle the challenges we are facing. Instead of getting trapped in the emotions of whose ideas are better suited, I realized that coming up with a "united" recommendation or recommendations is more advantageous than coming up with "perfect" advice that is not embraced by the team.

At home, this technique reminds me of being aware of the bigger picture when interacting with my daughter and my husband. Instead of getting sucked into the drama of emotions, it keeps me grounded in our family values and on what is important for the overall spiritual, emotional, mental, and physical health of the family—looking for opportunities for growth and learning. It supports me in being wise in my actions to not lose the forest for the trees.

2. Be Curious and Do Not Make Assumptions

Being curious and not making assumptions supports us in not losing opportunities for experiencing fulfilling interactions and for creative solutions to our challenges to emerge. We are not governed by our preconceived assumptions informed by our past experiences and what the future should look like. Being curious and asking clarifying questions behind each assumption helps shed light on what the expectations are and what success looks like for each party. This opens a realm of infinite possibilities as we are not in the confines of our preconceived assumptions and limitations informed by identification with the ego mind.

Asking clarifying questions during team meetings, I have witnessed teams make crucial adjustments for the best outcomes of the project. In many situations, the team was able to deliver ahead of schedule after challenging the existing assumptions. Questions bring to light the limitations the team is operating under and guide the team to explore possibilities that the team felt were initially not possibilities.

Challenging preconceived assumptions when working with people from different backgrounds and cultures supports us in taking the time to be fully present in the conversations with them. We will be amazed to discover we have more in common than not. This leads us to form lasting friendships and fulfilling relationships based on mutual respect and trust. In my personal experience, having one-on-one interactions and being present with team members has helped me understand their positions and expectations and the motivations driving them. In one instance, by asking clarifying questions, I was made aware that disagreement within the team resulted from one team member prioritizing the safety component and the other member focusing on the cost component of the program. This resulted in clearly capturing the assumptions and laying out the pros and cons before seeking senior management endorsement. The team members felt heard.

I have found this technique useful when implementing change and during crisis management. Taking time to clarify assumptions has assisted me in understanding resistance to change. In one situation, I found out that some of my team members were experiencing underlying fears of being judged, and the fears masked as resistance were causing them to blame the process change. This served as an eye-opener. Reiterating what the change was and what benefits would come from it helped senior management reframe the process change as a pilot experiment—one that would enable opportunities to improve on and adjust the process based on continuous feedback obtained from the team at fixed time intervals. This encourages a mindset to embrace change as an opportunity to evolve and grow instead of resisting change due to fears. It supports us in stepping out of the confines of our comfort zones to experience the miracles that await us.

3. Listen, Acknowledge, and Duplicate (L.A.D.)—Conscious Listening

Conscious listening is a vital part of being an ally, but it can be a hard skill to develop. As Stephen R. Covey once said, "Most people do not listen with the intent to understand; they listen with the intent to reply."

I first learned the Listen, Acknowledge, and Duplicate (L.A.D.) technique during my coaching certification, though I had learned the essence of this technique from my daughter, who was seven at the time. She helped me understand that when she shares her feelings and challenges with me, I don't have to advise her on everything. She wants me to listen to her without interrupting her. She wants me to be present with her—her feelings, her words that are spoken and not spoken—and listen to her with an open heart. When I started practicing this technique, it forced me to pause and tune into the nonverbal cues behind the words spoken. I tuned into the feelings behind the words. I acknowledged and duplicated how she was feeling, and that acknowledgment led her to feel heard and witnessed. Once she felt heard and witnessed, a portal opened, and she obtained clarity of potential solutions to her dilemma. I was amazed at how much more creative her solutions were than what I would have advised.

Most people during a conversation are preoccupied with what to say next instead of being present with the person in communication. The preoccupation is dictated by time constraints due to busy schedules, our prejudices, judgments, insecurities, our preconceived assumptions, our perceptions, and so forth. I have facilitated and been in meetings where members are talking over each other—sometimes unaware that other team members are still talking. This steals the opportunity for the team members to express themselves and feel heard. And when team members are not free to express themselves and feel heard, over time they stop contributing, and the team falls short of listening to diverse points of view and coming up with creative solutions. Creating a safe place to listen to the essence of what is being said includes noticing subtle nonverbal cues and body language, mirroring or reflecting in a genuine tone, and being open to refinement that confirms mutual understanding. The clarifying questions, responses, and communication follow from a place of curiosity and understanding. This opens the portal for effective and creative solutions to flow. Therefore, it is important to create psychological safety within ourselves so that we are present in the conversation and offer the same grace and a sense of psychological safety to others during a conversation.

This technique is effective when working with people from different cultures and where there are language barriers. I have been part of teams comprised of members from different parts of the world. I sensed a level of frustration where one of the team members had to keep repeating himself; he felt he was not being heard and not getting the needed information from the other team members. I pointed out this frustration to him at our one-on-one meeting. He had a follow-up individual conversation with the other team member, which led to clarity of the information required and received. He was satisfied and later acknowledged that patience and spending individual time with the other team member supported him in getting the appropriate information.

To sum up, the Listen, Acknowledge, and Duplicate (L.A.D.) technique emanates from a space of our coherent heart center when we are an ally to ourselves first and we show up with our replenished inner battery. We possess the energy to be fully present in our communication. This is an effective tool to use when communicating with ourselves, loved ones, clients, coworkers, and society at large, particularly during conflict and change management.

4. *Put Ourselves in Others' Shoes*

Putting ourselves in others' shoes cultivates qualities of empathy and compassion, essential components for designing creative, mutually beneficial solutions for the greater good of all involved. The solutions generated are genuine as they incorporate the empathy component. Empathy is tuning in and feeling with the perspective of the other person—how they spend their day and what challenges and obstacles they face each day. It stems from tapping into the empathy quality of self-allyship.

I learned this technique when I took a Design Thinking Workshop with IDEO U. The design thinking process clearly articulates the challenge at hand and gathers insights from end users, from people or caretakers close to the end users, or directly from what the end users are experiencing. For example, when discovering transformative therapies for patients with cancer, diabetes, Alzheimer's, or other diseases, it is impactful to put ourselves in the shoes of the patient living with the disease and experience what it feels like being a patient. Once we know what it feels like to be in the shoes of another, we brainstorm ideas based on gathered insights and converge ideas into practical themes or categories by building a prototype or solution, obtaining feedback from the end user on an iterative basis. This iterative communication process ensures that people impacted by the challenge are part of the creative solution process. It helps in developing effective solutions and products that are meaningful and readily adopted.

I experienced the successful application of this technique when I was part of a team responsible for designing best practices for working together based on trust, respect, and shared commitments to develop transformative therapies for patients. We conducted surveys, added focus group feedback, and participated in offsites to strengthen the partnership across the various groups. This resulted in not only designing and implementing best practices but also increasing both the quality of the deliverables and employee engagement because each group made an effort to put themselves in others' shoes.

This technique can be applied in our personal lives when we take time to switch roles for daily activities at home. For example, I am the sous chef, and my husband is the chef. One day when I was passing judgment (a.k.a. complaining about the food), my husband suggested we switch roles. It became my responsibility to come up with creative dishes, and I realized the time and effort involved in creating palatable dishes each day. This gave me a deeper appreciation for his loving contributions to our family.

I wondered if this principle could be applied to resolve conflicts on the world stage—at the country level and across countries where the stakes are so high. Leaders have many choices, but the choice to model and create psychological safety for a meaningful dialogue to occur creates the greatest impact. One such beacon of light was the South African leader and former president Nelson Mandela, who orchestrated a peaceful transition of power from the apartheid government. In his speech entitled "Africa and Its Position in the World Today" at the London School of Economics and Political Science (LSE) on April 6, 2000, he articulated, "Leaders who do not put the interests of their people above their own cannot achieve lasting peace and therefore sustainable development." He talked about the two conditions for peace. One condition is that all contending parties should be ready to participate in the process, and the other condition is a readiness on the part of all leaders to compromise by recognizing they have certain interests in common that are more important than the differences that divide them. Among those common principles is that it is totally intolerable that innocent men, women, children, and people with disabilities should lose their freedom and even be slaughtered because leaders cannot make the compromises required for peace. Therefore, as humans, it is important to discern between leaders who put their hidden interests above the interests of their citizens or employees, and leaders who put themselves in the shoes of their citizens or employees and stand up for what is in the best interest of everyone and with the intention of causing harm to none.

5. Do Not Treat Others as Objects or Means to an End

Like the ones before, this technique entails the quality of compassion. I experienced the essence of this principle when I went for a blood draw at a walk-in LabCorp clinic. Since it is a walk-in clinic, it is always crowded. The phlebotomist was experiencing difficulty drawing my blood, as I have tiny veins. She reached out to Marina, another phlebotomist, for help. Marina checked me out, and in her uncanny way acquired through years of experience, determined I had a deep vein somewhere below my skin. She got hot packs to warm me up and showed me how to relax my body. It worked wonderfully, and she was able to draw the necessary blood. I had a glucose tolerance test the same day that required me to come back to the lab after two hours. The time conflicted with Marina's lunch break. Without any hesitation, she told me to return and opened the back door for me to enter for the additional blood draw. Marina showed me what embodied compassion looks like. She treated me with compassion instead of as a number she had to quickly get through to meet the quota of patients she must see each day.

In contrast, one business owner of a small company had a celebration to recognize my friend for her contributions in helping the owner set up the business operations to generate a seven-figure profit. However, when my friend later asked for medical leave from work for eye surgery, the owner asked that she postpone her eye surgery. My friend said, "This surgery is not cosmetic. It's to address a life-threatening condition that, if not corrected, will lead to blindness." The business owner ended up firing her, saying, "I'll hire someone who will help me make double the profit." As long as my friend was able to provide value, she was celebrated. But when she needed to take care of her health, she was treated as an object to be discarded.

Due to our busy schedules and our desires to achieve and accumulate material possessions, we may unconsciously default to living our lives in old, programmed ways. But what if we take the time, even if it's for a few minutes each day, to be fully present in each interaction and relationship at home, at work, and wherever we go in our society? We consciously create an awakened society where giving and receiving love and compassion is the primary currency and the mode of operation.

Mother Teresa's quote rings true: "In this life, we cannot always do great things. But we can do small things with great love." Once, when I was sitting in the ICU waiting area,

I experienced people waiting patiently for updates on their loved ones, demonstrating kindness and compassion to each other. They listened to each other's struggles, provided comfort, checked on each other's needs, and prayed for the healing of their loved ones. My sister reached out to her work and friends to contribute to a support group created to offer financial relief to a mother whose son had been in the ICU unit for almost two months. I was in awe of the kindness and compassion demonstrated in the moment of crisis. I also remember a time when I moved aside in the grocery checkout line to make room for a woman carrying groceries in her hands. It took her by surprise, and she remarked, "Generally people are not so kind. This gives me hope."

When I read the mission and values statements of corporations, they frequently state that people are their most valuable and important asset. I wonder, though, if their decisions and policies related to their employees truly reflect that statement. I have been part of layoffs where we showed up one morning and could not access our computers. I have been fired with four months of severance after working with the company for over a decade. I felt hurt. When I was notified that one of my colleagues was fired, I reached out to see how she was feeling and let her know that I was available if she wanted to talk. On the other hand, I have been part of a layoff where the company provided its employees with ample notice, so we had the opportunity to map our transition plan.

I understand corporations have pressures to attend to their bottom line and demonstrate short-term success to secure the funds required to keep their operations running. However, when corporations ensure that their people practices, systems and infrastructures, products, and services are aligned with their values and mission, success is likely to follow. These principles create fertile ground for innovation and increase employee morale. When employees or people feel that they are not objects that can be discarded at the whims and fancies of the corporations, they feel more motivated to deliver. Employee engagement level goes up.

In one instance, I was having a challenging time scheduling a critical meeting due to upcoming holidays, vacation schedules, and travel conflicts. The team accommodated my meeting request to meet our program objectives with an early morning meeting for our US colleagues and a late-night meeting for our colleagues in Eastern Asia. This demonstrates that people will go above and beyond when they feel that they are valued.

6. W.A.I.T., Take Time to Reflect Before Responding, and Do Not React

In the hustle and bustle of our busy schedules, it serves us to pause to reflect on how our words and actions impact others and to be deliberate in using impeccable words (Ruiz Miguel, Don, 1997) and actions toward others. During my HeartMath Mentor Certification, I learned a "W.A.I.T." technique. "W.A.I.T." stands for "Why Am I Talking?" It is a reminder to wait before we speak. It is a reminder to sense and feel what is happening in the field around us—to genuinely tune in and listen to the essence of what is being said and know the difference between the words that were and were not said.

Similar to the L.A.D. technique, this is a part of conscious listening with a coherent heart.

John Donne wrote the poem "No Man Is an Island" in 1624. Today, our complicated social interactions with others continue to recognize the importance of Donne's message if we are to grow and develop as individuals and members of society. If someone upsets us, we may use the analogy that they have stepped on our toes. If the pain in our toe lasts longer than a moment, it may mean our toe was already infected, and the pain we feel may be rooted in our personal history rather than the person's less-than-perfect behavior. This does not excuse or condone the person's less-than-perfect behavior, but it points us to the place where we need to heal first by accepting, acknowledging, and witnessing our uncomfortable feelings. Once we witness our uncomfortable feelings, we can look deeper to understand if the intuitive uncomfortable feelings carry any wisdom for our growth and development. If so, we can become more emotionally stable. It helps to wait rather than respond to an email or a text immediately, or to excuse ourselves from a heated conversation when we are emotionally upset. This is an important element of responsible coherent communication.

Once we objectively process our feelings, then we set up an appointment with the person where we create a safe environment to share our feelings in a calm, mature manner. It is important to avoid blame and judgment and be rigorously honest about our feelings. Using first-party communication about how we feel creates an opportunity for the other person to understand how their behavior impacts us, which then allows them to reflect and modify their behavior if they choose to, as it is now part of their conscious awareness. Therefore, it is important to follow our feelings to the source during conflict or argument, center and stabilize first, and re-engage in the conversation later. This supports us in being an ally to others by being an ally to ourselves first. It is a mutually beneficial relationship.

When I was a little child, I recall reading this tale about a seller who rode his donkey from village to village selling women's bangles. He spoke to his donkey in a kind and affectionate way. Upon hearing him, onlookers laughed and questioned him, "Why do you talk this way to your donkey?" "You see, I work all day selling bangles to women," he replied. "They treat me like I'm their own. My tongue will develop the habit of speaking badly to ladies if I speak badly to my donkey. They will stop loving and respecting me." This tale left an impression on me and made me realize how crucial it is to develop the habit of using impeccable words toward all beings, including ourselves.

7. Give and Receive Concrete Feedback and Practice Forgiveness

Acknowledging and accepting responsibility for our dysfunctional conduct is the first step in providing and receiving feedback. It is a sign of our emotional maturity. It comes from the realization that we are all learning and growing, and our dysfunctional behaviors offer us an opportunity to reflect and grow. When we are willing to take ownership and correct our dysfunctional behavior instead of making excuses or getting caught in the blame and shame game, we are more likely to engage in coherent communication. We tend to waste a lot of time explaining our behaviors, which comes from the deep programming of our minds that we must be perfect to feel safe and be accepted by others. By acknowledging our dysfunctional behaviors, we realize it is okay to feel ashamed and embarrassed. By permitting ourselves to feel the uncomfortable feelings of shame and embarrassment, we allow ourselves to learn and grow from our experiences. We learn to fully love and accept ourselves for who we are. When we model this technique in our relationships and our communications, we foster a growth and learning environment that allows others to learn and grow from their dysfunctional behaviors.

People want things to change, but they are not willing to change. Our minds are happy to provide plenty of evidence and excuses for why we are not the cause of everything that happens. Nothing will change until we acknowledge and accept what is "as is." Our minds believe that we must fix everything around us so we can be happy and successful. When we muster up the courage to witness our own dysfunctional behaviors and see the whole truth as is without judgment, regret, or shame, then conscious, permanent, positive changes can occur. When we blame others, we give up our power to change.

This technique helped me build a spiritual relationship with my husband. I would get defensive each time my husband brought my dysfunctional behavior to my attention, coming up with a list of justifications to defend my behavior and listing his dysfunctional behaviors that were not relevant. This dysfunctional behavior kept me in the emotional loop of a blame and victim game. When I was able to witness my dysfunctional behavior and pause each time before responding, I was able to make gradual changes. An excellent spiritual partnership statement to make is "I will take care of me for you, if you are willing to take care of you for me" (Dalconzo, 2016b, p. 31).

Life is a learning experience whereby one cannot remain the same and still grow. As Nelson Mandela eloquently puts it: "Anybody who wants to have an impact on society must start from himself or herself."

This technique is effective when we are specific about our dysfunctional behaviors, including the context and impact, and when we avoid keeping score, instead articulating what we are willing to do to improve our behaviors. This opens up space for the other participants to own and correct their dysfunctional behaviors.

This technique serves us when we give behavioral feedback to others and when we receive behavioral feedback from others. When we are specific about the behavior, the situation in which it occurred, and the impact it caused, we do not fall victim to the blame, shame, and excuses game. During conflict and change management, this is a point of liberation, as the energy that could potentially have been expended in blaming, shaming, and making excuses is now potentially directed to creating solutions.

South Africa was a shining example of this during its peaceful transition of power. The South African government under Nelson Mandela set up the Truth and Reconciliation

Commission, chaired by Desmond Tutu, to help the country heal and move forward from despotism to democracy both by exposing the atrocities committed in the past and by achieving reconciliation with its oppressors instead of being engulfed in rivers of blood. In his book *No Future Without Forgiveness*, Tutu argues that true reconciliation cannot be achieved by denying the past. He presents a bold spiritual reminder that no matter how diabolical certain acts are, they do not turn the perpetrators into demons. He offers us the distinction "between the deed and the perpetrator, between the sinner and the sin, and to hate and condemn the sin while being filled with compassion for the sinner. The point is that, if perpetrators were to be despaired of as monsters and demons, then we were thereby letting accountability go out of the window because we were then declaring that they were not moral agents to be held responsible for the deeds they had committed" (p. 83). The commission operated "on the premise that people could change, could recognize, and acknowledge the errors of their ways and so experience contrition, or, at the very least, remorse and would at some point be constrained to confess their dastardly conduct, and ask for forgiveness. If, however, they were dismissed as being monsters, they could not by definition engage in a process that was so deeply personal as that of forgiveness and reconciliation" (Tutu, 1999, p. 83-84).

Reflecting on, acknowledging, and taking ownership of our dysfunctional behaviors, and practicing forgiveness for others' dysfunctional behaviors, fosters an environment of forgiveness and a growth mindset for others and ourselves. It highlights the Ho'oponopono prayer, which is an ancient

Hawaiian practice for forgiveness and reconciliation for both our and others' dysfunctional behaviors. Therefore, leaders who want to know what they truly believe should look at their organizations without rose-colored glasses to examine what they are mirroring. If they are mirroring dysfunctional behaviors, they can pause and ask themselves, "Am I unconsciously contributing to the dysfunctions of the organization?" If we think something outside of us is the cause of our pain or dysfunction, we'll look outside of ourselves for the answers. The outer world is often a reflection of what is happening within us. Therefore, owning our own dysfunctional behaviors creates room to take corrective actions and co-create the reality we desire.

8. Do Not Take Things Personally, and Maintain Healthy Boundaries

As I mentioned in Part I, under the spiritual and mental domains, maintaining healthy boundaries is crucial to being an ally to oneself. I now reiterate the importance of maintaining healthy boundaries and not taking things personally (Ruiz, 1997) in the context of how to be an ally to others.

This technique was demonstrated by my then seven-year-old daughter in her innocent ways. Two school incidents come to mind. The first instance, which she shared with her dad and me, occurred at school departure time. She said, "Mom, Dad, I have a private journal between my best friend Samantha and me. When school got out, I overheard Jamie saying that she was having her birthday party, and I asked if I could go to it. She answered, 'Only if you show me what's inside the journal.' I said, 'No, it's private between my friend and me, so I won't come to your birthday party.'" In a separate incident, my daughter dressed up in her African heritage attire with a headdress for her multicultural week at school. She told me, "Today at school, the boys were making fun of my headdress. But I didn't remove it. It's my culture and I'm proud of it." I secretly admired that she did not take the incidents personally, demonstrated self-awareness of her moral code, and responded with grace to the incidents.

I wonder if when self-awareness, self-love, and self-acceptance are engrained in our personalities and behaviors early in our childhood, we can be better role models to our families, the people we interact with, and society at large. I remember times as a child when I succumbed to peer pressure to fit in. I was afraid of standing out and not being accepted. This pretense may cause us to slowly lose the essence of who we are. We begin to lose what we truly believe in, what our values are, and what our moral compass is. We don't invest the time to learn and reflect on who we are as unique individuals. We grow up confused, accepting social norms, and feeling lost internally, and we end up being followers, pleasing others to be accepted, living a diminished life within our comfort zones, and dimming our unique light and unique talents.

I learned the distinction between a peacemaker and a peacekeeper from one of my mentors. She taught me that a peacekeeper fits in to be accepted and avoids conflict to maintain external peace, sometimes at the expense of compromising internal peace. In the process of fitting in and avoiding conflict, they betray themselves—who they are and how they truly feel. They are not honest with their feelings, and they carry the internal belief that they must please others to be accepted. On the other hand, peacemakers know who they are, their moral compass, and their values and truth. They possess the courage to stand up for what they believe in, in each of their pillars of life—personal, professional, social, and financial. They possess clarity of their spiritual, emotional, mental, and physical boundaries. They are firm about their nos and yeses. They are not afraid of speaking their truth or creating waves externally, even if it means it may upset others, because internally they are psychologically safe with who they are. They have healthy boundaries and do not take things personally. At a deeper level, they have a deep connection and trust in their innate guidance system that is all-loving and all-accepting. They are not enmeshed in other's beliefs, and they are not people-pleasers. In addition, there is a realization that others they interact with may not have the awareness of their Universal-Self—their innate guidance system, their inner potential, and their uniqueness. Therefore, the peacemakers do what is within their control: They model and live their truth. In doing so, they are an ally to others.

I experienced this distinction when I was taking care of my mom with my sister. My mom was recuperating in the hospital ward after nine days in the ICU. She was in a double room that was separated by a curtain. Soon a lady arrived with her husband to occupy the other side of the room. She was there for surgery. As soon as they arrived, they started complaining about the noisiness of the room, her bed not being next to the window, and the lack of attention from the nursing staff and the doctors. The husband rudely spoke to his wife. Their complaints intensified over the two days. They started comparing how my mom got more attention and asked why there were more family members allowed to visit her. My sister, who was quietly listening to the situation over the previous two days, broke her silence and assertively told the couple to stop complaining, and set out certain boundaries. It didn't matter to her when the couple complained to the administrative staff about her. She was clear about her boundaries and principles. To my surprise, I noticed a shift in the couple's behavior after the blowout. They were kinder to each other and to the nursing staff who were overwhelmed. To paraphrase Marianne Williamson in her book *A Return to Love* (1996), when we shine our light, we unconsciously empower others to shine their light. When we liberate ourselves from our fears, others are automatically liberated by our presence. Therefore, the embodiment of this technique helps us deal with conflict, change, and crisis management.

At work, I was aligned with a team member on the timing of a program strategy and asked her to facilitate a discussion at the upcoming team meeting in a month. She agreed. When I approached her a month ago to check their status, she answered that she had aligned with her manager, and they decided to push out the discussion for a few quarters. I was taken aback. When I set up a meeting to gain clarity, she declined and copied her manager. I was confused. To ensure everybody was on the same page, and the project was set up for success, I set up a meeting with her manager, the leader of the program, and her. During the meeting, I learned from her manager that their department was currently overwhelmed with competing priorities and hiring additional personnel. The insight I gained from the meeting was to not take things personally, especially as we may not always be able to see the entire picture, and our rational minds may not always understand the reasons behind people's behaviors. Therefore, taking the time to meet and clarify helped diffuse misunderstandings and judgments. This coherent technique supports us in being an ally to others while staying true to our boundaries.

9. Be Detached to Deal with Uncertainty

Like a fully opened rose, the detachment technique has different layers to it. Each layer offers its own wisdom and beauty of detaching and letting go of our ego-driven defenses, fears, worries, and need to control so that we can embrace the uncertainty as it unfolds in the present moment. As mentioned in the mental domain, the ego mind is attached to a rigid plan for how our lives should unfold. It seeks certainty and safety when, in reality, the zones of safety and certainty are always changing. Our rational minds cannot see and plan for everything.

When I was interviewing and applying for job opportunities, one of the companies on the US East Coast replied to me that it would be challenging to work with somebody from the West Coast due to a three-hour time difference. On the other hand, I was hired by a company where I collaborate not only with colleagues on the East Coast of the US but also with colleagues in Eastern Asia and sometimes in Europe. This experience provided me with the perspective that what one person perceives as an obstacle, another person perceives as an opportunity. Attaching to a rigid plan that lacks flexibility shuts down opportunities.

One of the humbling lessons I learned as a program manager over a career of nearly thirty years is that it is good to have plans and organize but not to get attached to the plans. I have been part of programs that were terminated as the strategic priorities of the organization changed. We learn to adapt and go with the flow as plans unfold in the present moment. Attachment to outcomes is a major cause of suffering for ourselves and others around us. Attachment prevents us from being present to the beauty around us, as we use the present moment as a means to an end instead of as the end goal itself. My training as a program manager has taught me to let go of my controlling behavior. Instead of being attached to the plans, I pivot based on the program and people's needs. When people see that we value them and know that we do not treat them as a means to an end, they will go above and beyond to value and support us. By detaching, we step into the field of infinite possibilities where events, plans, and people fall into place to realize our goals, our desires, and our intentions.

Detachment does not mean that we cannot be passionate about our ideas and opinions. It means that we cannot expect that others will have the same level of passion for our ideas and opinions. It means that we state our truth and present our ideas and proposals to others with passion but are not attached to how people receive them. They may not share the same enthusiasm and values as we do or be able to see what we see. History has taught us that great spirits have always encountered violent opposition. When we demonstrate psychological safety and emotional maturity, we do not unconsciously or consciously inflict pain and suffering on others when they do not support our ideas. We do not have our identities based on how others receive our ideas. We do not build resentment toward them, coerce them, or manipulate them. We accept them for who and where they are on their life's journey. This frees us to focus our energy on what we want to create—our intentions, our goals, our desires—instead of expending it on persuading others to accept our ideas. We believe in our ideas and take actions guided by our innate guidance system without attaching to outcomes.

At a deeper layer, the detachment technique teaches us to be allies to others by respecting their boundaries. This is true for our loved ones, our friends, our coworkers, and all with whom we interact. We gain the wisdom to allow the people we love to live their lives how they choose without any expectations that they satisfy us. This is a difficult realization, especially when we feel that we have solutions for people we love and cannot bear to see them suffering and struggling.

When I studied, practiced, internalized, and emotionalized the serenity prayer—"God, grant me the serenity to accept the things I cannot change, the courage to change the things I can, and the wisdom to know the difference"—I discovered the wisdom that my attachment and need to control events and people around me, no matter how loving or noble my actions appeared, originated from my fears of losing my loved ones and my fear of being alone. My ego mind was protecting me from feeling uncomfortable feelings of being alone, and I took on the savior role by stepping in and enmeshing myself by taking on the burdens and challenges of my loved ones. This profound realization and clarity supported me in discerning whether my responses and actions toward my loved ones, my friends, and my coworkers were originating from a space of deep love without expectations and without attachment to outcomes, or if they were originating from a space of fear, attachment, and control. I am learning to surrender my concerns, worries, and challenges to the inner guidance system that is part of my divine heritage. I trust that divine, universal, infinite intelligence and love are always working in my favor for my growth and evolution. I am learning to be an ally by not violating the boundaries of my loved ones, friends, and coworkers, with the realization that each of us grows by throwing our own gutter balls, making our own mistakes, and choosing to learn from the consequences of our own actions. I am embracing and leaning into the power of praying, surrounding my loved ones with the healing power of grace and love, and trusting the divine guidance on how to support them while respecting their boundaries.

Detachment is a lifelong process of making peace with the fact that everything happens for our own growth and development, even if it doesn't feel good (Dalconzo, 2016b). It is going with the flow of life's uncertainty. It is "being in the world and not of the world," as Jesus Christ eloquently said. Therefore, the detachment technique enlightens us through a deep understanding that when we are an ally to others, we are an ally to ourselves. This frees us to detach and enjoy our life journey of co-creation without resistance while allowing others to live their lives. Living with detached involvement is like being a lighthouse, living our purpose each day, being of service, and not being attached to any particular results.

In essence, detachment offers us profound growth and deep wisdom as it teaches us how the game of life is played. My daughter plays soccer competitively. On occasion, the team is asked to assist scrub teams in a tournament by playing as their guest players. Normally on the same squad, her teammates are now on opposing teams and facing each other. One time when this happened, my daughter silently prayed both for her squad lineup to contribute and for her personally to step up and go above and beyond to contribute. She didn't claim she would take all the shots, and she didn't worry about her team lacking the best players. She reflected this in her play. She inspired her team by setting an example. They shared the tournament's second-place finish. Detachment teaches us to accept the current situation as is and to be present to the infinite possibilities in front of us without getting attached to outcomes.

10. Smile, Laugh, and Don't Take Matters Seriously

My dad used to say, "Laughter is the best medicine." As I've gone through trials and tribulations, ups and downs, and the ebbs and flows of life, I've resonated with a phrase I once read: "Laughter is truth" (Tachi-ren, 2007, p. 134). A smile can lighten our day and the day of those around us. It is infectious. A good belly laugh is healing. No matter the struggles and dilemmas we are experiencing in our human incarnation, I find it amazing how laughter quiets the constant chatter of our thoughts, worries, burdens, and anxieties, healing our hearts spontaneously. It helps us detach from the narrative of our busy minds where we spend the majority of our time dwelling on our past, complaining about the present, or being anxious about our future. It supports us as we journey from the isolation of fear-based, protective, ego minds to the unified energy of our coherent hearts where we are connected to universal infinite love and the wisdom that pervades all things, always has our backs, and works for our highest good.

We realize laughter is truth when we wake up to the deep realization that the present moment is all we have and that we are *spiritual beings* in a finite body with a limited life span. Longevity is not a guarantee to anybody. When we realize this, we do not take life for granted; instead, we choose to smile as we know nothing is constant in the external world around us. We let go of clinging to people, circumstances, material possessions, and accolades. Instead, we choose to identify with the joyful, changeless Universal-Self within us. We ask ourselves each day, "How can I serve today? What will my legacy be today—a legacy of love, laughter, and faith or a legacy of separation, pain, and suffering?" When we align with a legacy of love, laughter, and faith, our vibrations increase, and we automatically radiate love, laughter, and light around us. We splash joy in the world as we experience joy in our lives. We manifest and co-create our realities with effortless ease as we synchronously align with the right people and circumstances in our lives. We learn to see the beauty and laughter in our challenges and develop a perspective that all our life challenges offer an opportunity to awaken and to embrace the divinity and greatness within ourselves and others. We develop a sense of humor. We lift others with our vibrations and are allies to others. We do not take life seriously, as we know that every challenge, too, shall pass away. We are transformed into witness observers of our human incarnate, realizing that we possess the wisdom to see beyond our human experience with the knowledge that we are not our body, our thoughts, our roles, or our past (Dalconzo, 2016b). We are co-creators of our lives in each present moment as we are connected to the universal life force energy reserves that connect us all in one spirit.

The following Transformational Affirmation is from my coaching certification. I use it as a reminder of how being an ally to others supports me in being an ally to myself.

> There is nothing in the world that exists that is not part of me, and there is no One who exists that is not a part of me. Therefore, any judgments my ego makes are Self-judgements, any criticisms that my ego levels are Self-criticisms, and any "projections" my ego makes are mirrored of what's hurting within me. This Self-mastered viewpoint has helped me to wisely extend to my Self and others, an unconditional love and acceptance that have increased my own and the world's Namaste Consciousness that we are all One in Spirit (Dalconzo, 2016b, p. 94).

Therefore, laughter is truth, and the punch line is unconditional love (Tachi-ren, 2007).

PART II SUMMARY

The true measure of being allies to others is when we wake up to the realization that our primary purpose in life is to give and receive love and to support each other to evolve and grow so that we become better versions of ourselves. When we are better versions of ourselves, we build a compassionate, loving society that is a peaceful, thriving, and prospering legacy for us and future generations.

Metaphorically, techniques on how to be an ally to others are like different facets of a diamond focused on demolishing the walls that separate us from each other and honoring the brilliant light that shines within us. We are united through our inner guidance system that pervades the universes and builds galaxies. It is omniscient, omnipresent, and omnipotent. We are unique manifestations of this infinite intelligence and compassionate loving guidance system that unites us. When we realize this fundamental truth, we love and accept who we are and who others are. We respect our differences.

We focus our energy reserves on responding to our challenges with grace and co-creating the reality and the life we desire. We are curious to discover ways of seeing beauty and learn from all forms of life and from all our triumphs and challenges. We wake up the child in us who shows us the delight in discovery. Over time, we are less governed by the conditioned responses of the ego mind whose primary responsibility is to build defenses and walls of separation to keep us safe and, in so doing, keep us from love and intimacy and from forming deep relationships. We learn to identify with and trust our innate unique guidance system whose primary responsibility is to unite us by breaking down the ego defenses so that we value and support each other to grow and develop.

The first five techniques of coherent communication listed under Part II share how to be an ally to others. Having a clear purpose and desired outcome in our conversations and interactions supports us in anchoring ourselves to what is unfolding in the present moment, which serves us in staying true to our purpose and achieving our desired outcome. The reminder of not making assumptions and being curious when interacting with others frees us from any of our preconceived notions and assumptions to discover the uniqueness of the other. It benefits us to listen to a variety of unique perspectives and lived experiences. This creates a fertile ground for rich conversations to occur and for creative solutions to conflicts and challenges to emerge. When we do not treat others as objects or the means to an end, we are aware of and appreciate the values and talents they have to offer and the contributions they make. We learn that people are not cogs in a wheel to be discarded after their use is done; instead, we ensure that the organization's practices, policies, and values genuinely treat people as valuable assets. The Listen, Acknowledge, and Duplicate (L.A.D.) technique teaches us to be attentive and listen with a coherent heart. We tune into the feelings, nonverbal cues, and body language behind the words spoken and the words not spoken. They teach us to be present with our body, mind, and spirit. We create a psychologically safe environment for others by acknowledging and mirroring how they feel. Putting ourselves in others' shoes cultivates the qualities of empathy and compassion, which are essential when communicating and creating mutually beneficial solutions. Once others feel heard and acknowledged, they feel appreciated and are motivated to go above and beyond to deliver their skills, talents, and resources for the benefit of the organization. Leaders who take the time to tune in and feel the challenges of their employees or their citizens will design solutions that are in the best interest of all involved.

The next five techniques teach us that by being an ally to others, we are being an ally to ourselves. This symbiotic partnership builds coherent communication and relationships. Acknowledging and taking ownership of dysfunctional behavior is part of the coherent communication giving and receiving feedback process, which is effective in conflict and change management and when providing and receiving behavioral feedback. It focuses on specific dysfunctional behaviors, the situations in which they occurred, and the impact they had. This avoids scorekeeping. We do not expend our energy reserves making excuses, justifying our dysfunctional behavior(s), or engaging in the blame game. This technique offers us the opportunity to learn and grow. We forgive others for their dysfunctional behaviors and do not hold any grudges. It offers us liberation as we can use our energy reserves to create effective solutions for the challenges we face and to co-create the reality we desire. The W.A.I.T. (Why Am I Talking?) technique ensures we are emotionally stable before engaging in heated conversations. When we are emotionally stable, we take ownership of our feelings, which allows the other person to modify their behaviors if they choose to. This way, we are being an ally to the other person by not using childlike ego defenses of shutting down or acting out.

By not taking things personally and maintaining healthy boundaries, we operate knowing who we are. When we do not compromise our values, or fall victim to circumstances, judgments, and the unconscious or conscious dysfunctional behaviors of others, we courageously shine our inner light and inspire others to shine their light.

Detaching from outcomes, ideas, and opinions is an effective technique for dealing with uncertainty. The underlying wisdom supporting the detachment technique is to trust and accept that whatever is unfolding in the present moment is for the greater good of all involved, as long as it supports growth and development. We learn to be passionate about our plans and take inspired actions without getting attached to outcomes or setting expectations about how others will support us. We learn to adapt, pivot, and go with the flow, trusting fully that the appropriate guidance and necessary support will always be provided for us. We learn to respect the boundaries of our loved ones, friends, coworkers, and all the people we interact with, with the understanding that each of us has the freedom and choice to learn and grow by throwing our own gutter balls. We detach from the rigid plans of how our lives and the lives of others we love need to unfold. We make peace with our truth and are loving and present for our loved ones, friends, and coworkers with detached involvement. Our hearts hold love and the spirit of service. We learn to see the beauty in our lives, in the lives of others, and in our surroundings as we detach from our fixed way of being. We do not take our lives or others for granted. We see infinite possibilities in life uncertainties.

Smiling, laughing, and not taking matters seriously helps us take a break from the constant chatter of our busy minds to dwell in the unified energy of our coherent hearts where we are one in spirit. We learn to be both a witness and an observer of our lives, asking the question "What is this experience, dilemma, or challenge teaching me?" We are an ally to each other in the transformational journey of growth. We realize that laughter is truth and the punch line is love. This technique offers us the perspective to view our life challenges as an opportunity to awaken and embrace the divinity within ourselves and others. We live our lives purposefully, waking up to the question "How can I be of service today?" We radiate love, laughter, and light to ourselves and others, as we identify with the joyful, changeless, boundless Universal-Self.

CONCLUSION

The key to coherent communication is to first be allies to ourselves by creating psychological safety within us and possessing the courage to be the authentic, unique versions of ourselves. This originates with us taking the time each day to build deep trust, identify with, and connect with the infinite intelligence, love, compassion, and clarity of our inner guidance system. When we feel psychologically safe, our hearts are coherent, our emotions are balanced, our autonomous and hormonal nervous systems are regulated, and we emit an aura that offers others the same sense of psychological safety to be an authentic version of themselves. This creates a ripple effect of transformation across all of humanity as our vibrations align with a frequency of love. This opens up space so that creative solutions to collective challenges can emerge. This enables the creation of societies built on deep respect, love, and compassion, where innovations and breakthroughs occur that uplift humanity. We create and model a legacy of love, deep appreciation, and prosperity so future generations can thrive.

Part I explored the techniques on how to connect to our Universal-Self through recurrent coherent practices in each of the four interrelated domains: spiritual, emotional, mental, and physical. Studying, practicing, internalizing, and emotionalizing the coherent practices in each domain imbues us with deep peace with who we are. We recognize the divine spark within us and awaken to our unique talents and gifts. We obtain clarity about our divine purpose. We realize we are never alone even in our darkest moments. We are enveloped with infinite compassion and universal intelligence guiding us in light and love. We speak and emit our truth, bearing witness to the patterns of our conditioned ego mind. We possess the courage to recognize our role in a conflict, and we take ownership of our dysfunctional behaviors and our fears. We cultivate a growth and learning mindset as we learn to unconditionally love and accept ourselves with all our perfections and imperfections. Recognizing our self-worth and the gifts of our talents and skills we possess to offer to humanity, we lead inspired lives co-creating the realities we desire with effortless ease. We respond to life's challenges and adversities with courage, grace, and ability, feeling empowered in each of our four interrelated domains. Our empowerment battery is fully charged so that we can be our strongest ally. We wake up each day with gratitude in our hearts asking ourselves, "How can I serve today using my unique abilities and strengths?" We experience the joy and grace of living in the present moment and recognize the beauty of each day.

CONCLUSION

Part II explores the techniques of how to be allies to others. We break down walls that separate us as we awaken to the realization that we are connected to each other through the same inner guidance system that builds universes and galaxies. We realize that our primary purpose is to support each other to evolve and realize the divinity within us. We forgive and let go of our pettiness, resentments, hatreds, and fears that divide us. This allows us to be fully present and communicate with our coherent hearts, where we are in full communion with each other. We realize that we can create miracles on earth when we come together with our unique talents. When we are an ally to others, the blessing we receive is multifold. It supports us in our journey to become an ally to ourselves and a better version of ourselves.

In writing this book, it is my heart's desire that you take the time to pause and reflect on how your Universal-Self is already working in your life and how you can invest the time daily to build a strong relationship and partnership with your Universal-Self. This empowers you to step out of your comfort zone and build strong partnerships with others. A simple act of presence and kindness each day toward ourselves and others we interact with can go a long way in fostering inner peace and joy.

The line "I am the monarch of all I survey. My right is none to dispute" from the poem "The Deserted Village" by Oliver Goldsmith resonates within me as I often pause and marvel at the great abundance and expansiveness of trees. Trees are in a constant state of giving to humans, to animals, and to each other. They are always in gratitude and service to the present moment. They appear to reap the fruits of their actions in the form of abundance many times over (Johnson, 2003). You and I are like trees that blossom in their season and bring forth their fruits.

Wishing you the very best in your journey to be the best ally to yourself and others. I am sending love from my heart to yours.

Coach Mona
monakjohnson786@gmail.com

REFERENCES

Caltech. (2023). *What is quantum physics? Caltech: Caltech Science Exchange Wordmark.* https://scienceexchange.caltech.edu/topics/quantum-science-explained/quantum-physics

Dalconzo, H. (1998). *Self-Mastery: A journey home to your . . . inner self.* Holistic Learning Centers.

Dalconzo, H. (2016a). *Seven spiritual truths to guide you back to your . . . inner self.* Holistic Learning Centers.

Dalconzo, H. (2016b). *The HuMan handbook: A guide book for the . . . inner you.* Holistic Learning Centers.

Dispenza, J. [@LeeWiggins]. (2013, February 8). *Dr Joe Dispenza-TED talks with Dr Joe Dispenza* [Video]. YouTube. https://www.youtube.com/watch?v=W81CHn4I4AM&t=4s

Duhigg, C. (2016). *What Google learned from its quest to build a perfect team.* New York Times Magazine. https://www.nytimes.com/2016/02/28/magazine/what-google-learned-from-its-quest-to-build-the-perfect-team.html?_r=0

REFERENCES

Goodreads. (n.d.). *Neil deGresse Tyson Quotes.* https://www.goodreads.com/author/quotes/12855.Neil_deGrasse_Tyson

Hunt, L. (1838). Abou Ben Adhem. *Poetry Foundation.* https://www.poetryfoundation.org/poems/44433/abou-ben-adhem

Institute of HeartMath. (2014). *Building personal resilience training manual: A handbook for HeartMath certified coaches and mentors.* https://www.heartmath.com/wp-content/uploads/2019/06/Sample-BPR-CM-Handbook.pdf

Institute of HeartMath. (2025). *Notice and ease tool.* https://www.heartmath.org/resources/heartmath-tools/notice-and-ease-tool/

Kaiser, L. (2016). *Maya Angelou: Little people, big dreams.* Frances Lincoln Children's Books.

Kemp, M. (2003). *Leonardo Da Vinci.* Oxford University Press. https://doi.org/10.1093/gao/9781884446054.article.T050401

Kishnani Johnson, M. (2023). *The power of universal laws: A parent/teacher guide to raising empowered children in four stages.* Balboa Press.

Morse, G. (2002). *Hidden minds.* Harvard Business Review. https://hbr.org/2002/06/hidden-minds.

Notable Quotes. (n.d.). *Mahatma Gandhi quotes.* www.notable-quotes.com/g/gandhi_mahatma.html

Ruiz Miguel, D. (1997). *The four agreements: A practical guide to personal freedom.* Amber-Allen Publishing Incorporated.

REFERENCES

Tachi-ren, T. (2007). *What is lightbody?* (3rd ed.). World Tree Press.

Tolle, E. (1997). *The power of now: A guide to spiritual enlightenment* (1st ed.). New World Library.

Tutu, D. (1999). *No future without forgiveness* (1st ed). Doubleday, Random House, Inc.

Walsch, N. D. (2005). *The complete conversations with God.* TarcherPerigee.

Williamson, M. (1996). *A return to love: Reflections on the principles of 'a course in miracles'* (2nd ed). HarperOne.

EARLY TESTIMONIALS

"Mona Kishnani Johnson's *Coherent Communication* has shifted me from the inside out. My experience has been prolific. I feel as if I have walked through a portal into everlasting support and internal fortitude. I am uplifted and forever grateful for the love of the Divine and Mona's wise heart. Her step-by-step guidance offers a deep and joyful practice with the potential to have profound realizations and revelations! I have been meditating as well as teaching meditation and meditative movement for many years in addition to other modalities that promote a peaceful existence. As someone who never stops learning, I am in awe of the sense of inner serenity *Coherent Communication* imparts to its reader. It offers the real meaning of life and how to live it fully empowered! Mona navigates courageously into the abyss of Infinite Intelligence and Divine guidance for every human and soul. As she stated, 'We discover that we are the spark of the divine system, that we are spirit first with a mind and a body, and that we have the innate ability to use the limitless energy reserves of our guidance system to co-create the reality we desire and deserve.' Thank you, Mona, for offering us your beautiful and inspiring legacy of work."

—Edwina S. Ferro, 500 E-RYT Integral Yoga Teacher, Bay Area Meditation & Spiritual Guide, and mother of two

"Working in People & Culture, I found this book to be an essential guide for creating a healthier, more supportive workplace. The idea of being an ally to yourself first, before extending support to others, is profound yet often overlooked. The line 'After all, we can only give others what we already possess' beautifully underscores how self-compassion is the foundation of genuine allyship. By being kind and gracious to ourselves, we open the door to more empathy and deeper connections with those around us. The book's emphasis on extending grace—first inwardly, then outwardly—speaks to the core of meaningful communication and collaboration, ultimately fostering stronger, more resilient relationships."

—Melissa Merrick, People & Culture / Head of Human Resources

"Mona Kishnani Johnson has created a wonderfully detailed guide to improving self-awareness and awareness of others in the pursuit of a better understanding of the motivations of others and ultimately improving communication. Ms. Johnson guides us through methods and examples of how we can first learn to appreciate our own selves, improve our sense of self-awareness, and become our own 'best ally.' She then leads us through using that understanding and thoughtfulness to learn to better understand, empathize, and especially become better able to communicate and share thoughts and perspectives with others. Ms. Johnson uses many examples throughout this book to clearly illustrate issues and the techniques needed to resolve issues in a manner in which anyone can easily relate. This is an easy read that can have dramatic results on many levels."

—Kenneth Sansone, Pharma/BioTech Professional

www.ingramcontent.com/pod-product-compliance
Lightning Source LLC
Chambersburg PA
CBHW070635030426
42337CB00020B/4018